THE ISTHMUS ZAPOTECS

A Matrifocal Culture of Mexico

Second Edition

BEVERLY NEWBOLD CHIÑAS
California State University, Chico

CENGAGE
Learning™

Australia • Brazil • Japan • Korea • Mexico • Singapore • Spain • United Kingdom • United States

CENGAGE
Learning™

THE ISTHMUS ZAPOTECS: A Matrifocal Culture of Mexico, Second Edition

BEVERLY NEWBOLD CHIÑAS

Executive Editors:
Michele Baird
Maureen Staudt
Michael Stranz

Project Development Manager:
Linda deStefano

Senior Marketing Coordinators:
Sara Mercurio
Lindsay Shapiro

Production/Manufacturing Manager:
Donna M. Brown

PreMedia Services Supervisor:
Rebecca A. Walker

Rights & Permissions Specialist:
Kalina Hintz

Cover Image:
Getty Images*

ISBN-13: 978-0-03-055057-7

ISBN-10: 0-03-055057-2

Cengage Learning
5191 Natorp Boulevard
Mason, Ohio 45040
USA

Cengage Learning is a leading provider of customized learning solutions with office locations around the globe, including Singapore, the United Kingdom, Australia, Mexico, Brazil, and Japan. Locate your local office at:
international.cengage.com/region

Cengage Learning products are represented in Canada by Nelson Education, Ltd.

For your lifelong learning solutions, visit **custom.cengage.com**

Visit our corporate website at **cengage.com**

Printed in the United States of America

This book is dedicated to my parents,
Lewis F. Newbold and Glennie A. Newbold
and to
My Beloved Friends Dolores and Concepción

Foreword

ABOUT THE SERIES

These case studies in cultural anthropology are designed to bring to students, in beginning and intermediate courses in the social sciences, insights into the richness and complexity of human life as it is lived in different ways and in different places. They are written by men and women who have lived in the societies they write about and who are professionally trained as observers and interpreters of human behavior. The authors also are teachers, and in writing their books they have kept the students who will read them foremost in their minds. It is our belief that when an understanding of ways of life very different from one's own is gained, abstractions and generalizations about social structure, cultural values, subsistence techniques, and the other universal categories of human social behavior become meaningful.

ABOUT THE AUTHOR

Beverly Chiñas is Professor Emerita, Department of Anthropology, at Chico State University, Chico, California. She received her M.A. degree in 1965 and her Ph.D. in 1968 from the University of California, Los Angeles. The fieldwork on which the original case study was based took place from July 1966 to late November 1967. Since that time Dr. Chiñas has continued to investigate the roles of Isthmus Zapotec women, returning to the community for six months in 1975 and for another six months again in 1982–1983. Between these longer periods of fieldwork she has spent from a month to six weeks in the field during many summers over the past 24 years. Her latest period of fieldwork comprised four weeks in November 1990. The revised edition of *The Isthmus Zapotecs* incorporates data from the later periods of fieldwork in addition to those data collected during 1966–1967. Unless the year of fieldwork is noted in the body of the text, the ethnographic present is 1966–1967.

Of her early life experiences, which led her to a career in anthropology, Dr. Chiñas states: "I was born and raised on the Nebraska prairies, which were then, and to a certain degree still remain, the Nebraska of Willa Cather. Having no playmates, I entertained myself with imaginary Indian children as fantasy companions while I roamed the hills and bluffs of my father's ranch where Plains Indians had hunted bison less than a century earlier. Other peoples and other cultures have fascinated me since I first met them through the pages of the *National Geographic* magazine before I could read. When I finished high school during World War II, there was no chance for further education. I worked as a stenographer in civil service for several years, married, and began raising a family. I read everything I could find on history and anthropology and spent vacations year after year in the Southwest among the Navajos, Apaches, and Pueblo peoples. I wanted desperately to learn more. Secretly I entertained thoughts of undertaking college studies fulltime, but it seemed so wildly impossible that I could not bring myself to discuss it with my family.

"When my daughter enrolled in kindergarten in 1958 I finally found the courage to inquire about courses in anthropology at the local college. The next year I enrolled fulltime, majoring in anthropology, but it was not until I received my B.A. and a scholarship to graduate school that I could bring myself to tell anyone outside the immediate family that I was doing anything more than 'taking a few courses at the college.'

"I have tried always to impart to students some of my enthusiasm for anthropology and especially to convey the excitement and adventure of fieldwork in an exotic culture. Women's roles have been one of my great preoccupations since I became aware of some of the ambiguities of such roles in our culture about the age of twelve.

"Other abiding interests have been biology, geology, ethology, and creative writing. For fun I jog, bicycle, watch the birds and other wildlife in my garden, and travel. Since 1985 I have bicycled across France, through southern China, down the Natchez Trace, in the San Juan Islands, Canadian Rockies, and Canyonlands, Utah."

Dr. Chiñas initiated and taught a course in women's roles cross-culturally from 1972 to 1986. She has also taught courses in peasant cultures, anthropology and development, Mesoamerican and South American ethnology, Latin American Studies, and cultural anthropology.

During the past few years Dr. Chiñas has devoted increasing time and energy to environmental causes, especially to promoting the bicycle as an ecologically sound alternative transportation mode for the United States and many other countries.

ABOUT THIS CASE STUDY

This case study is written by a woman and stresses roles assigned on the basis of sex, with particular emphasis on women's roles. Beverly Chiñas, quite properly however, places this emphasis upon sex roles in the context of a wide-ranging descriptive analysis of salient features of Isthmus Zapotec culture.

As she points out, anthropological descriptions of cultures have been biased by the dominance of male anthropologists working through male informants in cultures where interaction between the sexes is subject to a great many restrictions. Many highly regarded ethnographies do indeed depict women as though they were a part of the background. The foreground is occupied by men carrying on public roles as hunters, head men, and honor seekers. Many reports, even some using sampling procedures, have failed to separate the sexes and the data relevant to each. In our research with the Menominee and the Blood Indians, and in our current work in Germany, we have found it to be imperative to treat males and females as representing two potentially quite different universes. As Dr. Chiñas points out, other anthropologists have found this to be of critical importance as well.

Her model for the analysis of sex roles emphasizes the distinction between formalized and nonformalized roles. She correctly regards the formalized roles as constituting the most visible, but quantitatively the smallest, part of the total role structure of the cultural system. The formalized roles, which are most often occupied by men, particularly in their public dimensions, have been most frequently described because they are manifest and because they are formalized. The nonformalized roles are frequently left unexplicated, thus giving a distorted perspective on the whole behavioral system and the complex of expectations and demands that lie behind behavior.

In this new edition Beverly Chiñas stresses the matrifocality of Isthmus Zapotec culture. She points out that the mother is *structurally* central to the family "probably everywhere in the world", but not always *culturally* central, which requires that the people "hold an ideal of the mother role as central to the functioning whole of the culture". She is also "affectively central"—emotional ties between mother and child are the strongest in the family. Zapotec women exercise strong economic, social, and kin-related power and authority, and relations between husband and wife tend to be strongly egalitarian. Chiñas does not leave the claim of matrifocality at a generalized level but gets down to specific cases and behaviors in situations where women take action with tacit or explicit consent from others that could occur only if the mother role was central. Women not only take action that influences the behavior of other women but they also intervene in the affairs of men, particularly when violence is likely to occur if nothing is done to prevent it.

A new chapter on *muxe* ("man–woman"), "transvestites", "cross-dressers" describes a third-gender role between men and women. Some, but not all, are homosexuals, but all take some of the characteristics of the other gender. Chiñas explores Zapotec (in San Juan) attitudes toward this third gender of persons, and toward other forms of variation in sex roles, including lesbianism, masculinized women, and bisexuality.

A new chapter on changes between 1967 and 1990 concludes the case study. Much of what was in place in 1967, the date of the author's first field study, is still in place, but demographic, technological, and environmental developments are accelerating, particularly since the large Pemex oil refinery in the nearby port city of Salina Cruz began operation. Not all of the changes have been positive. A wholesale degradation of the environment has taken place as a result of oil spills and air pollution related to the refinery. Since the refinery will be nearly doubled in capacity shortly, conditions will probably not improve in the foreseeable future. The role of women, as well, has not improved as a result of modernization and technological change, as is often the case.

The reader will enjoy this case study not only because it has an interesting and significant focus, but also because it is lively in its description and balanced in the treatment of various aspects of culture, including subsistence, life cyle, religion and ritual, social and sex role behavior, and relations to the changing social, cultural, and physical environment.

LOUISE AND GEORGE SPINDLER
Senior Editors
Calistoga, California

Preface

For the anthropologist, the first major fieldwork experience is akin to the initiation rites which young people in nonliterate cultures must often "pass" in order to become adults. The "elders" have prepared the budding anthropologist as best they could in classroom, seminar, and simulated or limited field experiences near at hand. Finally, the novitiate conceives and designs a research project and presents it to a fund-granting institution. Providing the institution considers her project worthy and funds are available, the initiate eventually finds herself actually "in the field", ready to begin the first major undertaking of her career.

In my case "the field" was the Isthmus of Tehuantepec, Mexico. As is usual, I arrived there uninvited, unannounced, and unexpected, as naive as a small child concerning the correct modes of behavior in Zapotec culture. Although I spoke and understood Spanish, I was totally unfamiliar with Zapotec, the first language of most of the inhabitants. Since more than half the population were bilingual, it was my plan not to spend months learning Zapotec but rather to hire a bilingual local person as interpreter when needed.

The first couple of weeks passed quickly. I sought out important local persons such as the *presidente* (mayor) of the town—introducing myself, explaining my project, and asking for his cooperation. I looked for suitable quarters where I could both live and work with relative efficiency at the rather formidable task of recording, organizing, and analyzing field notes and data as accumulated. Because my project centered around women's market activities, I spent considerable time loitering in the several markets of the region, at first mainly observing since I had not yet obtained enough information to formulate the questions I wished eventually to ask. The Isthmus dialect of Spanish is so heavily laced with Zapotec intonation and phraseology that I initially found it difficult to understand, but that situation improved rapidly. I succeeded in finding an ancient but spacious house only a couple of blocks from the main marketplace, for which I signed a three-month lease, although the rent was triple the amount I had budgeted from my modest living allowance.

The size of the marketplace in El Centro seemed more amenable to the research efforts of a lone (and lonely) field-worker than that of neighboring San Jacinto, and this fact, plus convenient quarters, led to my decision to concentrate efforts in El Centro.[1] It is doubtful that I could have found a more unpleasant, malodorous marketplace in all of Mexico.[2] The main structure, purported to date from the

---

[1]Throughout the case study, place names are changed where it seemed necessary to protect the privacy of informants. Fictitious names are substituted for all persons, except historical personages, for the same reason. Words that appear in the glossary are italicized and translated only the first time they are used.

[2]A new market structure was completed in the mid-1970s. In 1990, sanitary conditions in the "new" market were not greatly different from what they were in the old market in 1966.

1840s, was buried in the heart of a patchwork of annexes, arcades, expansions, and alterations that had been accomplished at various times over more than a century. The result was a cavernous interior with incredibly poor light and ventilation, crowded with two- or three-hundred women vendors and customers, sundry stray dogs, and a rather astonishing array of fresh and decaying produce, flowers, meat, fish, and poultry, as well as every description of nonperishable food product, yard goods, clothing, housewares, and hardware. The combination of scents that greeted the unwary market entrant were, at first, so overwhelming as to prove nauseating. But I soon struck upon a game that served to divert my attention as I entered each morning until my nose became accustomed to the unfamiliar odors. The "game" was nothing more than trying to distinguish the individual sources of the various intermingled odors, some of which were quite agreeable when considered singly.

During the first weeks I familiarized myself with the names of products and their sources, an activity that seemed innocuous and was easily elicited from the women vendors. I spent a couple of weeks mapping the interior of the main marketplace and its outdoor annex. Reports had led me to anticipate considerable suspicion and hostility, but these failed to materialize at first. People apparently assumed that I was only a curious *turista* (tourist) who would soon disappear. When that did not occur and I began sketching the market's layout, people began to display increasing curiosity about my motives. I answered all questions as truthfully and comprehensibly as possible, explaining that I was making a study of the Isthmus markets, the products bought and sold, the sources of products, and characteristics of the vendors for the purpose of writing a *tesis* (thesis) as part of my training to be a teacher. This was understandable to at least some persons, except for the fact that I, a "rich *Gringa*" (woman from the United States), had come all the way from my country, alone, to study such a poor, simple thing. The word went around (without my knowledge at this point) that I was a spy. That was, after all, the only logical explanation for my continued presence and my preoccupation with the market place, its activities, and its personnel. I was a spy "for the government," sent to gather information for the purpose of increasing taxes! It was not long before a few women refused to answer my questions. More women joined them. In a very few days the general attitude of the market place was hostile, even though two or three women continued to be cooperative and friendly and tried to smooth out the difficulties on my behalf.

The armed market watchman asked if I had permission to ask questions. I whipped out the letter of introduction from the presidente. The moustached guard, looking precisely like the sinister *soldado* (soldier) of Mexican western films, spat on the floor and said my letter was worthless. There was now a new presidente and I would have to obtain *his* permission.[3]

Since I had the support of a few people, I thought it best to try to weather the storm. Doggedly each morning I entered the marketplace with a bright (forced) smile. Just as doggedly my most vocal adversary, an elderly *señora* (married lady) whom I am sure thought she was doing a great service to her people, mounted the counter of her *puesto* (market stall) and began her long and loud harangue against

---

[3]The first presidente, I learned, was only an interim official appointed by the governor to fill the office until a disputed election was settled.

me. When conditions did not improve within a few days, I decided my temporary absence might lower the anxiety level which continued to build among the market women. The time could be well spent making a survey of other market places in Oaxaca, Chiapas, and Veracruz for comparative purposes.

In my absence the spy story hit the front page of a regional weekly. I was now reported to be a "Yankee imperialist" spy whose government had a vital interest in the region as the site of a new interocean canal! The reporter suggested that immigration authorities might be interested in my case and that I would probably be deported henceforth. Fortunately, the spy story had already run its course by the time I returned, and I was gradually able to resume work in the marketplace. Eventually I obtained the cooperation of most of the previously hostile women, some of whom later apologized for their discourteous treatment and invited me to visit them in their homes.

Soon after I began working in the marketplace, I discovered that buying a small quantity of some unfamiliar food item and then striking up a conversation about it with the vendor was a pleasant way of establishing rapport. I continued this practice as I resumed work after the "spy scare." Often the purchase was something I could share with the women themselves, several of us sampling the food together on the spot. A favorite place of the *tortilleras* (tortilla sellers) was around the perimeter of the venerable central fountain, the old-fashioned kind with a basin around the bottom to hold the fountain's water. Dogs drank from the basin frequently. I never imagined that the basin also served as the only source of potable water for the entire marketplace. One morning after sampling a bit of fried dough, which I had shared with two tortilleras, I casually bent over and rinsed my fingertips in the basin. A dozen loud voices protested, catching me completely by surprise. I must have looked as puzzled as I felt when I asked the woman beside me what I had done wrong. "You washed your hand in the fountain and that's bad. That is the water we use for cooking and washing dishes." Properly humiliated, I made profuse apologies, promising to abide by rules of the marketplace in the future if known to me. That incident broke the ice. Women smiled and began talking, asking me questions about my family, my home, my clothing, and my country. It occurred to me that at least I need not worry about Isthmus Zapotec women laughing at my mistakes behind my back as is the case in some cultures. No, indeed. These women, one could be certain, would point out all my mistakes immediately and directly. Their candor and frankness were surely among their most enchanting and refreshing characteristics. Rapport with the women improved steadily thereafter as I assumed the role of naive student of *las costumbres* (the customs), not at all a difficult role at this point, and they were placed in the more rewarding role of teacher.

But if relations with the women improved, there were other problems that continued to plague me to the end. One of these was obtaining official data or information, as the following excerpt from my daily record indicates:

3/3/67   Went to El Centro at 8 A.M. First went to Palacio. I told Secretary Romero, "Well, this is the day I was to return." "Oh, what may I do for you, señorita?" "Do you have the census data?" "Census? No, but I can order the book from the library for you ahorita." "No, Señor Romero, it's the census data that the *maestros* (teachers) and students collected last month that I need." "Oh, did they make a census?" (This after he had promised a week ago to get it for me pronto!) "Yes, Señor Romero, they did and I understood that your office had the data." "No, señorita, I don't know anything about it, but let me talk to the director of the school." "Thank you, Sr. Romero, but that's not necessary. I can speak to him on my way home." (Director wasn't in.) After six months I am still waiting for the first delivery of any promised data from anyone!

This afternoon I went to house of Maestro Muñoz, who had promised census data for San Juan Evangelista a month ago. He wasn't there but same old story. His wife said: "Oh, was there a census??????" I told her I could pay for whatever time was required to get the information. "But it's very easy. It only takes a few minutes. It isn't necessary to pay." We visited for an hour. Maestro Muñoz didn't arrive.

Frustrations there were, but there were often humorous situations, too, and some that seem more humorous in retrospect than when they occurred. For example, this terse note from my daily record:

Saturday, 2/4/67 As promised I took Bilma and Panchita to *el campo* (the fields). All the Gallegos children, another girl, and a couple of miscellaneous *niños* (small boys) went along (not as planned). I hit a bad hole and Roberto's head broke the camper window, but his head is intact. This is the last time children ride in the back! Bilma told me her *huertas* (gardens) were very near, right by the cemetery. They are five miles away. She said the road was good (it is barely passable). In addition I foolishly didn't wear slacks and am covered with *sancudo* (local tiny but vicious mosquito) bites.

Or the following, recorded as part of a visit to the sick mother of a friend:

1/17/67 I was feeling pretty good this P.M. (had been sick) so I went over to Xadani to see when Aurelia wanted to go to Tabasco. . . . The conversation turned to curing. Chica said she heard there's a gringa who lives in Mixtequilla, who prescribes the two hind legs of a cricket be put in the bed with the patient to cure backache and she thought they should try it for her mother (dying of cancer). I asked if she needed crickets (I have plenty) but she said no, she had *un montón* (a pile) at her house too. Don't suppose anyone would be interested in several hundred bats or a couple of fat iguanas either!

When my three-month house lease expired, the most urgent work in the central marketplace was completed. I wanted to become more intimately involved in neighborhood life in order to gain a better understanding of family, kin, and neighborhood social interrelationships. I rented a smaller house just at the entrance of San Juan Evangelista, where most of the traffic entering and leaving this pueblo, mainly afoot, passed my door. Slowly over the months that followed I learned something of the ways of Isthmus Zapotec culture—with the help and guidance of a great many kind and patient "teachers." I patterned my actions and responses as closely after my neighbors as possible. At first I played the new roles consciously and superficially. Especially in ritual situations—wedding fiestas, funeral rites, fiestas to the saints, and such—when the expected behavior was completely unfamiliar to me, I carefully followed the women's behavior patterns. When they knelt, I knelt, when they prayed, I tried to pray in the same words, and when they paid their *limosnas* (ritual contributions), I did likewise. Gradually the correct responses, the expected behavior, began to become internalized and automatic. Before I left my many good friends and my adopted family at San Juan Evangelista, I felt I was at least a small part of the way toward becoming a *Juaneca* (woman of San Juan).

To the Fields by Oxcart, Author and Friends (1990)

The people permitted me to share with them many hours of dull routine (which were seldom dull for me), as well as moments of intense joy, sorrow, and despair. A few individuals selflessly came to share my own hopes, confidences, and small moments of triumph and defeat. Those many hours of listening and talking, the unstructured research one does simply by living with people, were among the most informative and rewarding of all. I hope my Zapotec friends remember those times with equal pleasure.

I went to the Isthmus as a stranger, but a stranger I shall never be there again. On the many occasions since 1967 when I have returned to work and visit, someone has soon welcomed me with, "Ay, Bevi, !Que milagro! You've come home." It is a sentiment I cherish and proudly share.

Acknowledgments

It would be impossible to thank each of the many individuals to whom I owe much for help in fieldwork and in completing this case study. The initial fieldwork could not have been undertaken without the generous assistance of the National Science Foundation (GN 1064). Fieldwork in 1975 was accomplished through the generosity of California State University in granting me a sabbatical leave, while 1982 fieldwork was possible through another sabbatical and Wenner-Gren Grant 4253.

Especially profound is my debt to the late Dr. Ralph L. Beals of the University of California, Los Angeles, who encouraged me in the formulation of the original research project and offered advice and moral support throughout. I am also indebted to George M. Foster of the University of California, Berkeley, for his helpful comments from time to time when the case study was in the planning stages, and especially for his reading and advice on the original case study outline. Several of my colleagues at California State University, Chico, have graciously and patiently acted as a sounding board and have unfailingly given of their time and support. Students have provided their own unique form of support in their enthusiasm and interest in my fieldwork and in Isthmus Zapotec culture. A very special thanks goes to Lucinda Triffo, my graduate student assistant in 1982, who proved to be not only an exceptional assistant but also a good friend to both me and the people of San Juan.

To my friends in the Isthmus of Tehuantepec, for their graciousness as my hosts and teachers, this case study is an inadequate but sincere expression of my great admiration and gratitude. Although I cannot identify them individually, many will recognize themselves in the pages that follow. My deepest debt is to my dear friends, Doña Dolores and Conchita, both of whom died within six months of my 1967 departure. Their trust, empathy, and intelligent assistance, so generously and selflessly given, are responsible in large measure for whatever insight I was able to gain into life in San Juan Evangelista during the earliest fieldwork. ¡Qué Diós les quiera!

BEVERLY NEWBOLD CHIÑAS
Chico, California
January 1991

Contents

List of Illustrations

THE ISTHMUS
ZAPOTECS

A Matrifocal Culture
of Mexico

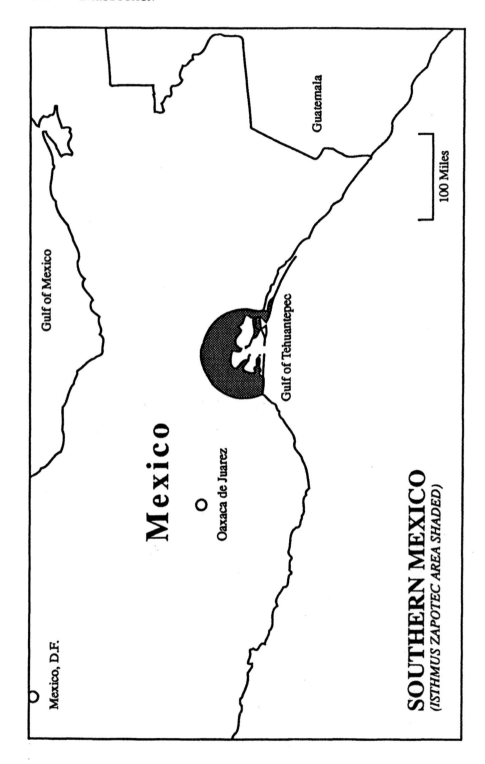

SOUTHERN MEXICO
(ISTHMUS ZAPOTEC AREA SHADED)

Introduction

Anthropologists have usually described the cultures they study by focusing on men and men's roles, not particularly because anyone planned it that way but rather because such an orientation was the logical outcome of male anthropologists working through male informants in cultures where interaction between the sexes is subject to a great many restrictions, prescriptions, and taboos. In *The Isthmus Zapotecs* I try to "correct" this time-honored tradition, not because I believe women are more important than men in Isthmus Zapotec culture but because they seem as valid a focal point as men, and one too long neglected.

The Isthmus Zapotecs is not a study only of the women but of a matrifocal cultural system and women's roles within it. My goal is to present the reader with an image of the ways in which the roles of the sexes are mutually dependent and complementary in terms of everyday living, not only in the economic division of labor but in every aspect of the social system.

Since anthropologists research and analyze whole cultures (the holistic approach) and women are part of the whole, they have always been included in anthropology to some extent. Too often, however, women have been presented ethnographically in a curiously impersonal, dehumanizing way—as shadows moving in and out of the important and engrossing activities of men or as objects whose main functions are to serve and to be manipulated by their menfolk (fathers, brothers, husbands, and sons). The women have seemed to be passive, mindless creatures as colorless as fog. If ever such a presentation reflected women's views of their culture, it must certainly have been the rare exception. Probably more than a little of our own cultural bias is involved. Prior to the 1970s the same emphasis on men and male activities could be viewed nightly on national television networks, appearing perhaps in its purest form in the ubiquitous western.

Focusing on male roles in other cultures is not confined to male anthropologists of course. Women anthropologists have often done likewise, selecting research problems which center around male roles in the first place because, as a colleague recently explained it, "that's where the action is." The truth of her statement undoubtedly lies in how one chooses to define "action"; yet whatever the answer, the fact remains that women as culture bearers and as approximately one half of the participants in every culture deserve more attention than they have traditionally received if we are to gain an adequate understanding of that enormously complex whole we call culture.

Part of the problem of dealing effectively with women's roles has surely been the tendency to evaluate them in terms of male roles. If one defines "action" in terms of what males do, then indeed male roles are "where the action is." Roles assigned on the basis of sex are often complementary, but not comparable. One of the first rules of logic teaches us that comparing things that are dissimilar leads to

1

A Hilltop Home (1990)

invalid conclusions. But where sex roles are concerned, the comparisons are too often implicit, as are the assumptions derived from them. Perhaps we have over-looked the "action" of women's roles in many cultures because it is qualitatively different from that associated with male roles.

Among the assumptions that appear to underlie too many ethnographic descriptions, two seem particularly crucial to the study of women's roles. The first assumption is that the sexes perceive their culture and their own sex's place in it in essentially the same way. The second assumption is that men and women share a common culture on similar terms. A number of anthropologists have suggested that such assumptions are almost surely invalid, varying perhaps in degree of invalidity from one culture to another. (See, for example, Elkin 1950, Friedl 1967, Mintz 1969, and Spindler and Spindler 1970.) For the great majority of anthropologists up to about 1970, however, sex roles did not attract much interest. Since that time a new generation of anthropologists with a keen interest in sex roles (or more properly, roles assigned on the basis of sex) has systematically addressed themselves to a reexamination of the issue. The results of their efforts are now incorporated into mainstream anthropology and have contributed mightily to our knowledge of sex roles and their variations cross-culturally. If *The Isthmus Zapotecs* has contributed in some small way to an understanding of gender roles in a specific culture and to gender roles generally, I am grateful for having had the chance to make such a contribution.

Anthropologists, though, have only recently begun serious research on sexual and gender variations although such phenomena often have been noted and briefly mentioned in ethnographies from around the world. Following that tradition, I duly noted and casually mentioned Zapotec sex/gender variants several times in the first edition of *The Isthmus Zapotecs*. I did not offer more information because (1) I had not intentionally gathered such data and, therefore, did not have much confidence in the miscellaneous observations I had made and (2) because it did not seem to me that I could present such material to readers in the then homophobic United States so that they could understand and accept it as part of everyday Isthmus Zapotec culture. As a result of the so-called Gay Movement our attitudes here in the United States, at least in a portion of the population, have broadened regarding sex and gender anomalies. Many of us no longer view the world as dichotomously male or female but realize that there are degrees of maleness and femaleness in each of us and that these sex/gender traits express themselves differently in each individual. In the twenty-plus years since the original research, I have gained more information about Isthmus Zapotec attitudes toward sex/gender variations, and I have included that information in the present edition (see Chapter 9).

Turning attention to the case study, one of the most difficult tasks has been to describe Isthmus Zapotec culture briefly but in sufficient detail to convey an accurate image of the culture and the people. A culture presents many images, all of which may be equally accurate, but none of which taken alone describes the culture. Every anthropologist is forced to discriminate and select, both in recording his data and in reporting. What I report here is only a part of Isthmus Zapotec culture. If it is not that part which my many Zapotec friends and informants would have preferred, I offer apologies. Much of the cultural heritage of which they are so justly proud—their music, poetry, dances, traditional ceremonies, and their role in national history has been recorded by others. A readable English language account of the region and the various ethnic populations of southern Mexico is *Mexico South* by Miguel Covarrubias, first published in 1946.

To facilitate an understanding of the part of Isthmus Zapotec culture reported in these pages, I employ two devices. The first is an analogy of the culture and its many strata to the earth viewed through a successive series of overlay maps. In the first overlay Isthmus Zapotec culture is perceived only superficially, in broad outline, somewhat analogous to viewing the earth's surface from an altitude of thousands of feet, where some of the surface features can be seen but without fine detail. As we proceed to subsequent levels of culture, different features are revealed at each level, which allow us deeper insight into the culture just as peeling away pages of an overlay map of the earth would reveal different features of the earth's composition at each level. Limitations of time, space, and knowledge allow us to view only a few of the cultural overlays. We leave to the reader the task of reintegrating in her own mind the various cultural levels presented. If I have done my job well, the reader should be able to "get the feel" of Isthmus Zapotec culture from these pages.

The second device is an analytical model of roles that I believe is useful in explaining and describing sex roles in Isthmus Zapotec culture. *Role* is here defined as a "bundle" of rights and duties associated with a particular status position. Every individual holds a number of statuses simultaneously and fills the roles associated with each status presumably to the best of her ability and understanding. But types of roles differ. Some are formalized to such an extent that every adult member of the social system knows the "bundle" of rights and duties the role demands even though he will never be expected to fill the role. Others are what I refer to as nonformalized, or roles that are not so clearly perceived or rigidly defined by members of the society. Perhaps we can conceptualize the totality of a social system as an iceberg, with the formalized roles representing the part that floats above the waterline—the visible part—and the nonformalized roles as the submerged but larger portion. The formalized roles lend themselves to description and analysis precisely because they are formalized. Thus, these are most often the roles described by anthropologists and sociologists. Crosscutting the formalized–nonformalized dichotomy is another structural distinction that I shall refer to as private and public domains. The private domain refers to the basic social unit of the society, the family or other domestic group. The public domain refers to everything outside the basic social unit. This double dichotomy, formalized–nonformalized roles and private–public domains, yields four types of role distinction: (1) public formalized; (2) private formalized; (3) public nonformalized; and (4) private nonformalized.

Universally, public formalized roles seem to have been dominated by men. That is to say, the large majority of such roles are defined by the culture as male roles. Private formalized roles, on the other hand, usually seem to form complementary pairs by sex and are therefore often approximately equally divided between the sexes. Undoubtedly both sexes also function in many nonformalized roles, both public and private, but much less is known about these because they are not readily visible to the social scientist. Perhaps nonformalized roles outnumber formalized roles in all social systems, or maybe there is much variation from one social system to the next. At present, we simply do not know.

Man Off to the Fields (1990)

In Isthmus Zapotec culture, women often hold nonformalized complementary roles in the public sector for which men hold the formalized roles. To what degree this may be true in all cultures is another unknown. Speaking only for the Isthmus Zapotec social system, knowledge of women's nonformalized roles appears to be as crucial to an understanding of the total system as is knowledge of the formalized roles of men.

Role distinctions in terms of the model are explained more fully in Chapter 8. First, we must become familiar with the various cultural overlays—historical, ecological, and social—that form the background for Isthmus Zapotec role behavior. Here is the stage on which the people of San Juan Evangelista interact as they seek to gain a livelihood, meet their familial, social, and religious obligations, and find some sense of personal satisfaction in their daily lives.

The aims of the case study are two: (1) to present a reflection of life in San Juan Evangelista that stresses the interdependency of the sexes and the complementary nature of their roles; and (2) to impart to the reader a sense of Isthmus Zapotec women's nonformalized roles and their centrality to the functioning of the social system.

Having used *The Isthmus Zapotecs* in teaching about women cross-culturally for nearly 20 years, I have had time to reflect as to how I would present the material if I were writing it for the first time today. Because the first edition appeared at the very inception of the comtemporary Women's Movement in the United States and the concurrent revolution of social science research and theory on women, there were then few shoulders on which to stand theoretically. Today, in all the social sciences, including anthropology, there are large pools of new research and theory concerning women which have helped me to gain more insight into, and to appreciate all the more, the Isthmus Zapotec culture. I now consider the Isthmus Zapotecs a matrifocal culture, as defined by Nancy Tanner, and the only indigenous matrifocal culture known in Latin America. My theoretical reorientation is reflected in the new subtitle of this revised, updated edition.

1 / Wind, Water, Mountain, and Plain: The Physical Setting

The Isthmus Zapotecs are the southernmost branch of a large population speaking several dialects of the indigenous language, Zapotec, and located in the state of Oaxaca, Mexico. Although the state is ethnically highly heterogeneous, Zapotec speakers have long been, and remain, the majority population of Oaxaca. Since pre-Contact times, 150 miles of rugged mountains have formed a barrier between the Isthmus Zapotecs and their linguistic cousins in the Valley of Oaxaca and in the sierra. This moutainous barrier has insulated more than isolated the Isthmus Zapotec population from the other Zapotec-speaking populations so that the dialects have become mutually unintelligible, for the most part, and other cultural distinctions have evolved, mostly related to environment and subsistence patterns.

In national usage "El Istmo" refers only to the Pacific coastal plain of the geographical Isthmus of Tehuantepec, a distinction observed throughout this case study because it defines the area occupied by the contemporary Isthmus Zapotecs and their ancestors for at least a thousand years.

The climate of El Istmo is tropical and semiarid by definition, although one gains the impression of severe desert-like aridity or lush verdancy, depending on the season. The brief rainy season, late May through October, is marked by sudden torrential storms that cause a good deal of soil erosion and flooding. Although official records indicate that rainfall averaged 32 inches per year between 1956 and 1965, the nature of the rainfall and the porosity of the soil make effective rainfall considerably lower. Nonetheless, the rainy season is generally a pleasant time in El Istmo. Breezes freshen and become gentle, the inescapable dust is briefly stilled, and agricultural work lessens to the degree that water and mud make it impossible. With the first rains of the season, yesterday's brown hills spring to life with tropical abandon, trees and bushes burst into flower, and roadsides turn velvet green. On fields without irrigation, crops have been carefully planted just before the rains to take full advantage of the short wet season. With luck, maize will be mature by the end of October when the rains cease. The violent wind, *el norte*, returns with the end of the rains, skittish and uncertain at first but soon ceaseless and raging, merciless in its onslaught for half a year.

November and December are called the cold months by *Istmeños* (native Isthmians), a time when one might need a sleeved garment or a light wool *rebozo* (shawl) in the early morning hours before dawn. Soon after the cessation of the rains the countryside is again brown and dead, the hills and *el monte* (scrub forest) covered with spinous, xerophytic scrub interspersed with a few leafless deciduous trees. Starkness and desolation prevail, relieved only by the irrigated strips and splotches that remain lush through the long dry season, lending an oasis-like character to the landscape.

Since earliest occupation, two forces, wind and water, have molded Isthmus Zapotec subsistence patterns and culture. The destructive power of el norte has dictated the location of most Zapotec settlements behind or between the few hills that dot the coastal plain, affording a degree of protection from its relentless attack. Although native low-growing crops such as maize and cotton probably demanded minimal wind protection, the modern fruit crops of bananas and mangoes cannot be grown successfully except in the few microniches afforded by river valleys and the leeward side of the hills. This fact has led some intra-Isthmian agricultural specialization involving these fruits.

Water, however, has probably been more important to the people over the long run than has wind. There is considerable evidence that the Pacific coastal plain has been gradually desiccating over the past century. Perhaps it is a trend of much longer duration, In any event, within the memory of people still living, a number of families in San Juan Evangelista could supplement their incomes by fishing and collecting fresh water shrimp from the rivers and lagoons of the *municipio* (county); but today, most of such places have either disappeared entirely or are so sporadic and seasonal that they no longer support edible marine life.

For a long time irrigation has been very important to Isthmus Zapotecs. Small-scale river valley irrigation was almost certainly practiced in pre-Contact times, although the earliest documentation known to me occurs in 1580 (Torres de Laguna). Almost as important as irrigation have been the seasonal inundations of rather extensive areas of the coastal plain during the rainy season when rivers and streams pour thousands of acre-feet of water out onto the plain from the vast watershed of a mountainous hinterland. While crop damage and flooding of dwelling sites have been frequent results, the silts carried by the flood waters have also provided a natural source of fertilizer, rendering many fields perpetually productive. A government irrigation and flood-control project which began operation in 1964 has made year-round irrigation available to much previously unproductive land, but it also has eliminated the possibility of seasonal inundations. One result has been the necessity of applying expensive commercial fertilizers on fields to maintain fertility. Another result unfavorable for *juanecos* (inhabitants of San Juan) is that what remains of the river has now become a putrid, threatening open sewer instead of a source of food and recreation.

The two most prominent features of the Isthmus landscape are the mountains and the coastal plain. The Pacific plain, perhaps 20 miles in breadth at its widest point, is stalked by majestic segments of the imposing mountain chains that parallel the Pacific Ocean the length of two continents. Somewhat less formidable here than farther south, the mountains are nonetheless impressive as they rise abruptly behind the plain. Isthmus Zapotecs are plains-dwelling people. They avoid the mountain hinterland so much a part of their landscape as a dread and dangerous place. Stories circulate of carnivorous creatures, some mythical and perhaps some real, inhabiting the mountains, lying in wait for human prey. The hinterlands immediately sur-

Central San Juan from a Hilltop (1990)

rounding the Istmo are not uninhabited however. Since before Contact various ethnic groups, including Mixe, Zoque, Chontal, and others, have occupied the area, trading mountain products for Zapotec and Huave products of the sea and plain. These people, known collectively as *serranos* (mountain dwellers), are familiar to the plains-dwellers; and some Isthmus Zapotecs have migrated to the mountain communities to raise coffee, displacing the older population almost entirely in a few cases and thus becoming serranos to the remaining plains-dwellers.

Other linguistic and ethnic groups have been present although, in historical times, Zapotecs have always been the major population group of the area. One of these other ethnic groups, the Huaves, who speak a language as distinct from Zapotec as African Bantu is from English, may have occupied the area when the first Zapotecs arrived from the north, about A.D. 1000 or earlier. Today the small Huave population lives in several settlements on the sandspits of the Pacific Ocean. Probably their total population is no more than 5,000. By comparison, approximately 57,000 Zapotec speakers are listed in the 1960 Censo General, of a total Isthmus population of approximately 97,500.[1] The percentages of Zapotec speakers vary by

[1]The 1990 census figures are not yet published, but it is clear by observation that the past 30 years has seen a steep increase in population in the Isthmus as elsewhere in Mexico. Although families have become smaller, population growth continues because of the sheer numbers of people of child-bearing age. In the Isthmus there has been an influx of non-Zapotecs to some cities such as Salina Cruz as a result of petroleum-refining operations. The 1960 figures are only approximate because the census figures are compiled on the basis of *ex-distritos* (a political division encompassing several municipios). The two ex-distritos of the Isthmus include forty-four municipios, all but eleven of which are outside the traditional Isthmus Zapotec area. The figure of 57,000 for Zapotec speakers was probably much too low even in 1960 because Zapotec is the low-status language compared to the national language, Spanish. In any case, using genetic rather linguistic criteria, the percent of the population that is Zapotec would probably surpass 90 percent in the eleven Zapotec municipios.

municipio from only 13 percent in Salina Cruz to 96 percent in San Juan Evangelista, the average being approximately 60 percent. Somewhat more than half of all Zapotec speakers also speak Spanish, a figure that can be expected to continue to rise as school attendance increases. The Isthmus also contains a sizable population of persons who speak only the national language. This group, approximately 40 percent of the total population, reflects two ongoing processes with a long history in the Isthmus: immigration of non-Zapotecs into the area and acculturation of Zapotecs into the national culture through formal educational process and exposure to outside influences. Since language is the main criterion of ethnicity, Zapotecs who learn only Spanish as children are classified as non-Zapotec in the government census even though they may be Zapotecs genetically.

Not only ethnically, but culturally and socially as well, the Isthmus of Tehuantepec is a mosaic of complex patterns. Some peoples speaking totally unrelated languages have quite similar cultures and life styles, as for example, Zapotec and Huave *campesinos* (farmers). Within the Zapotec-speaking population itself, on the other hand, one encounters a full range of social and cultural variation—from the poor illiterate campesino who speaks little or no Spanish to the wealthy, educated professional person (often a lawyer or an engineer) as urbane as any upper class citizen of the nation's capital. Basically, the Isthmus Zapotecs are still largely of the social type defined anthropologically as peasant and as such are in many ways comparable to peasant populations in other parts of the world. It is this majority peasant Zapotec population that forms the basis of the case study.

Many Isthmus Zapotecs retain a great deal of pride in their cultural heritage. Some Zapotec elites, both in the Isthmus and in the national captial, have tried to encourage retention of the native language and ethnicity. Some of these individuals compose songs and poetry in Zapotec, often publishing them at their own expense, while others take pride in recording for posterity certain of las costumbres that are gradually disappearing from people's lives and memories. Popular songs in Zapotec are composed by local musicians also and are introduced to the public at fiestas. Some of these have become very popular regional songs. In these ways, Isthmus Zapotecs seem to be unique among Latin American indigenous populations. To my knowledge, no other ethnic or linguistic group in Mesoamerica currently produces literature and music in the native language.

2 / Binni Gula´sa´: Prehistory and History

PREHISTORY

Binni gula´sa´ are the ancient ones, familiar to every Isthmus Zapotec through the frequent chance finds of ancient cultural materials. From time to time, informants report discoveries of urn burials, tripod pottery, very large *ollas,* and small stone figurines. Habitation sites are numerous but difficult to date from surface material, which includes small obsidian points and tripod shards in the form of serpent heads very similar to those from Yagul, Valley of Oaxaca. A large carved stone lintel, also with serpent head motif, lies half buried in debris beside the oldest church in San Juan Evangelista. Few people are aware of its presence and none knows its origin. A few months after I left the field in 1967, a man excavating for a house foundation on a hilltop uncovered what was reported to be part of a *templo* (pre-Contact religious structure). All of these things were left by the binni gula´sa´, say the people, and the binni gula´sa´ are the ancestors of the Isthmus Zapotecs, they believe. But that is a question even archaeologists cannot answer, for a great many different peoples have inhabited or passed through the Isthmian corridor for thousands of years, peoples whose languages cannot be determined from the archaeological record. The Pacific coastal plain must have served as a funnel for foot travelers between North and South America from the first, as people found the Gulf coast with its immense meandering rivers, swamplands, and dense tropical growth impassable.

Several habitation sites on the coastal plain excavated by Delgado (1961) revealed pre-Classic cultigens of maize, squash, and cotton as well as the remains of wild boar, badger, deer, turtle, shrimp, and a variety of birds and fish.

By glottochronology, Isthmus Zapotec language separated from the mother tongue about seven centuries ago, a date supported by recent archaeology at Mitla and Yagul, Valley of Oaxaca.[1] Since modern Isthmus Zapotec language is also more closely related to the Mitla dialect of Valley Zapotec than to others, it is reasonable to postulate the Mitla–Yagul area as the point of origin. Perhaps the Huaves occupied the coastal plain when the Zapotecs first entered the Isthmus, and

---

[1]Glottochronology is a method, developed by Morris Swadesh, whereby elapsed centuries since the separation of two or more related languages can be estimated through statistical analysis of cognates. The method assumes a similar rate of change for all languages and a constant rate within a single language, which has led to criticism. However, archaeology and other dating methods lend strong support to its reliability regarding Isthmus Zapotecs.

were gradually displaced to their present marginal position at the edge of the Pacific by an expanding Zapotec population, a postulate still unverified.

Situated on a mountain high above the Tehuantepec River is the only well-known and impressive archaeological ruin of the Isthmus—Guiengola. For many years it was thought to have been constructed in the fourteenth century as a fortification against the Mexicas,[2] but archaeological investigations have revealed occupation of the site intermittently by various peoples, beginning in the Archaic Period (7000–3500 B.C.). Later levels contained Zapotec ceramics and Mayan figurines, which Forster dated as contemporary with Monte Alban III (Forster 1953).

HISTORY

In 1496, Zapotec–Mixtec forces defended the Isthmus against Mexica attackers from the venerable fortress, Guiengola, in a siege that lasted seven months. Finally, according to tradition, the Mexica gave up in defeat. Some of the Mixtec allies decided to remain in the Isthmus, founding the settlement of Mixtequilla which still exists at the foot of the mountain (Iturribarria 1960).

When the Spaniards arrived in 1523, El Centro was already a sizable settlement. The region was governed by Cosijopii, son of the Zapotec ruler of Zaachila, Valley of Oaxaca. Despite the reported defeat of the Mexica at Guiengola in 1496, the Spaniards found the Isthmus as well as the Valley and Sierra Zapotecs tributary to the Mexica (Gay 1980).

Once established in the Valley of Mexico, Cortes lost little time in turning his attention southward. Alvarado passed through the Isthmus on his march to Guatemala in 1523, renaming the largest settlement Villa de Guadalcazar, a name that endured through the colonial period (Cajigas 1954). In 1526 Cortes himself journeyed to the Isthmus, hoping to find a natural waterway from the Pacific to the Atlantic. His plan was to explore along the Pacific coast, search for the waterway, and perhaps even send an expedition across the Pacific. He came prepared, with men and equipment, to build and outfit seaworthy ships. Two ships were constructed eventually and floated on the great lagoon at San Mateo del Mar, only to be wrecked by el norte before they could put to sea. Later attempts proved more successful. In 1529 Diego de Ocampo sailed from the Isthmus to Peru, and other ships built here eventually sailed as far as the Molucas in the Pacific and to Baja California.

The Isthmus Zapotecs apparently offered no immediate resistance to the Spaniards. Cosijopii allowed himself to be converted to Christianity during Cortes' visit and was baptized Don Juan Cortes. At the time of his conversion, Don Juan held an estate befitting a king—an estate that included, among other amenities, a sylvan retreat at the foot of the mountains consisting of extensive gardens and a residence built around a natural pool formed by a great bubbling spring. Don Juan magnanimously demonstrated his zeal and loyalty to the new religion by donating most of his considerable estate to the Church, but could not bring himself to part with the beautiful retreat. That remained in the royal family until his daughter, in a similar

[2]Mexicas are popularly referred to as "Aztecs."

burst of Christian devotion, donated the last remnants of the regal estate to the padres some years later. In 1528, Cortes received from the Spanish crown the title of Marques del Valle de Oaxaca along with a vast grant of land, which included the greater part of what is today the state of Oaxaca. The immediate post-Contact years were marked by a decimation of indigenous populations of the Isthmus as dramatic as that reported for other regions of Mesoamerica. A population of 20,000 in 1550 declined in thirty years to 3,200, according to Torres de Laguna (1580). Certainly the 30 years before 1550 were no less critical. Then slowly after 1580 the population decline was halted and the trend gradually began to reverse itself. Some population experts believe that recovery to pre-Contact levels was not reached until the present century, 400 years after the first wave of devastating European diseases swept over the New World.

San Juan Evangelista was almost surely a community before the Contact. When it first appears in historical documents in 1543, it is a *barrio* (subdivision) of El Centro, and that may well have been true from its beginning. In the year mentioned, the Dominican friars were constructing the cathedral and convent in El Centro. Don Juan Cortes "ordered the barrio of (San Juan Evangelista) which was made up of fishermen, to bring to the Dominicans and workers daily sufficient fish to feed eight people and their servants," reports Burgoa (Gay 1980). Today it is no longer possible for residents to earn a livelihood by fishing, but that change is so recent that some people still remember the dugout canoes, the breechclouts, and the type of nets used by fishermen when they were children.

Independence and Revolution, the Macrovista

No other specific mention of San Juan Evangelista is known until the mid-nineteenth century when it reenters the pages of history as a *pueblo rebelde* (rebellious community), an epithet which lingers still, to be thrown out in anger on occasion.[3] But there are recorded incidents during the intervening three centuries in the Isthmus as elsewhere of uprisings and insurrections among peoples dominated by the Spanish crown.

A few clues to Zapotec social structure at Contact remain in scattered but tantalizing glimpses of the past, which permit us to suggest that even then, more than 400 years ago, Isthmus Zapotec women were active economically and in defending their pueblo. It is possible that the culture was strongly matrifocal before the Spaniards arrived. Among the clues, we know that noble women could own property and apparently dispose of it as they wished. Burgoa states that in about 1553 Princess Magdalena, the baptized Christian daughter of Cosijopii, donated to the Dominicans "the salt beds of Tehuantepec, her fields, a fruit orchard half a league in length, her recreational baths consisting of crystal springs which watered the orchard and formed a beautiful pool at a place four leagues from 'la villa' called 'Loayaga' " (Gay, v.1:405). At the time, Magdalena's father and two brothers were still living—her father confined to prison for harboring the elderly pagan priests

---

[3]It is probable that local government documents and records would yield additional information for the existing lacuna between 1540 and 1850 with reference to San Juan Evangelista. Unfortunately, these sources have not been open to researchers.

from Mitla and for practicing pre-Contact rites involving turkey sacrifices. He died soon afterward.

Another early reference relates to women taking an active part in political protest (as they do to this day). About the Tehuantepec Insurrection of Holy Week, 1660, which has gone down in history as the beginning of a much wider uprising, Gay takes from the manuscripts of Fr. Leonardo Levanto the following (Gay v. 2:230) (emphases added):

> At the signal (a loud whistle), everyone, Indian men and *Indian women,* arose en masse, abandoning their market stalls and merchandise where they had been working since early morning and, amidst fearful war whoops, began throwing stones of all sizes at the house of the alcalde major. . . . The prior of the convent went into the plaza and pleaded with people to stop but to no avail. They retorted that he should retreat unless he wished to die and because he did not retreat as rapidly as they desired, *three Indian women* and one Indian man overpowered him and pushed him into the entrance of the cemetery.[4]

Before it was over, the houses of the Spanish authorities had been sacked and burned and the alcalde mayor and three others stoned to death and dragged through the streets.

In his excellent compilation of the history of political resistance in the Isthmus, Campbell chronicles some nine rebellions of the region between 1660 and 1882 and cites mention of the deeds of heroic women in published historical accounts in at least five of these. How many other times through the centuries Zapotec women took an active and aggressive part in political protests, one can only guess; but it is a safe bet that they were seldom passive bystanders. Clearly, the people of San Juan did not become rebeldes overnight, nor were they alone in their fight against what they perceived as oppression by foreigners.

Around 1850, for example, the political situation in the Isthmus was such that the people of the barrio of San Juan found themselves opposed to the leaders in El Centro, who held the political power. The El Centro leaders, claimed the people of San Juan, were outsiders interested only in the exploitation of the Zapotec population (and, chances are, they were just that). Although most of the dozen or more barrios of El Centro were as Zapotec as San Juan, only the Juanecos found the courage to resist decisions originating in El Centro. Perhaps their location behind the mountain made control by El Centro officials more difficult than was true for the more vulnerable central barrios. In any case, between 1846 and 1868 San Juan repeatedly allied itself with San Jacinto, some 30 kilometers distant, to oppose El Centro political control. It was a time of great political turmoil on a national level, and local issues were often national issues. At least once, the Juanecos were able to establish themselves briefly in the *palacio* (city hall) of El Centro, and at least once, San Juan was sacked and burned by its opponents, its people forced to flee into the countryside or seek refuge with their San Jacinto allies.

The climax came in 1867 when San Juan and San Jacinto allied themselves with Loyalist Porfirio Diaz to resist the French Intervention while El Centro joined the pro-French Imperialists (Cajigas 1954). At last, the Juanecos were on the winning side.

---

[4]Translation and emphasis mine.

During Diaz' long regime, 1876–1910, the Isthmus of Tehuantepec apparently enjoyed comparative peace and prosperity, the latter reaching a peak with the opening of the port of Salina Cruz in 1894 and the completion of the trans-Isthmus railroad in 1907. With the railroad came instant fame and fortune, locally called the *Epoca de Oro*, because the Isthmus of Tehuantepec was the shortest trade route between the Atlantic and the Pacific oceans. As many as fifty trains traversed the Isthmus daily bearing international cargoes, and there was a great influx of all types of persons hoping to capitalize on the boom. But, alas, it was all too brief. Only seven years later, the Panama Canal opened and the Golden Era of the Isthmus of Tehuantepec died as suddenly as it was born (Cajigas 1954).

There are many historical accounts of the stormy mid-1800s and of the Mexican Revolution (1910–1920). The Zapotecs were heavily involved in these political upheavals. The Isthmus, one must remember, has always been politically and militarily strategic by its geographical nature. The Zapotecs provided their share of generals, war heroes, martyrs, and traitors: and their homeland has been no less a battleground in the history of Mexico than have the more famous battlefields of the north.

Independence and Revolution, the Microvista

Zapotec historians recount history somewhat differently from national historians, and oral traditions of historical events often emphasize points overlooked or unknown on the national level. One point is clear: History lives for the Isthmus Zapotecs in a very vital and personalized way. Juanecos especially hold Porfirio Diaz close to their hearts. He is their great hero of Mexican Independence. After a century, illiterate campesinos can point out spots where Diaz and his men camped, and they take great pride in recounting Diaz' personal interest and affection for Juanecos. "He promised to do anything for his friends, the Juanecos, and he always kept his promise," they state, these men who did not learn history from books. To Juanecos, Diaz' greatest deed was granting the status of independent municipio to San Juan Evangelista for its efforts against the French. History probably records otherwise because Benito Juarez, not Porfirio Diaz, was head of the national government at that time, 1868.

Local historical tradition is interesting also in the strong, heroic role it records for Zapotec women who sometimes fought beside their men but more often smuggled messages and supplies through enemy lines and provided key information about enemy plans and movements. Actually, we now know such roles were not unique to women of the Zapotec region during those turbulent years, but they may well have played a stronger role in the Isthmus than elsewhere. Regardless of the historical facts, what is interesting is the importance attached to women's roles in historical events recounted by Isthmus Zapotecs themselves. Where historians on the national level neglected to mention women's heroic deeds or recorded the deed but not the name, Zapotecs personalize their history with the names and kinship relations of heroic women and men with equal fervor. Perhaps this is no more than history personalized, but it may be another manifestation of that elusive quality of relationships between the sexes which has led more than a century of casual observers to perpetuate the myth of an Isthmus Zapotec matriarchy.

I use the word "myth," because anthropologists have never encountered any truly matriarchal cultures, i.e., cultures in which women's roles are the mirror image of men's roles in patriarchal cultures. Yet the idea of matriarchy goes back to the very beginning of anthropology to Bachofen, Westermark, and others who mistook matrilineal descent for matriarchal rule. The myth of matriarchy is still perpetuated in non-anthropological literature as fact although anthropologists have been trying to set the record straight on the non-existence of matriarchy for 60 years or more. In popular Mexican culture and in travel guides the Isthmus Zapotec is still erroneously referred to as matriarchal. Not until the 1970s was a type of culture recognized where women do hold a central, but different, place than men: the matrifocal culture.

3 / San Juan Evangelista Today

ITS RELATIONSHIP TO THE LARGER COMMUNITY

The pueblo of San Juan Evangelista is the focal point of this book, but like all human communities, it does not exist in isolation. San Juan has very close ties with the wider Isthmus Zapotec community and cannot be accurately described except in the wider context.

The two largest communities of the Isthmus Zapotecs, El Centro and San Jacinto, are approximately 30 kilometers apart and contain between 40 and 50 percent of the total regional population. There are a number of other, smaller towns, several with populations well over 5,000. Few people live in dispersed homesteads in the rural areas, even though perhaps the majority of Zapotecs are campesinos. For centuries they have been town dwellers and that is the mode of life they prefer. However, it is a mistake to think of Isthmus towns and cities in terms of towns and cities of the United States. They are quite different, having few of the amenities we tend to associate with an urban environment. Isthmus Zapotecs, however, conceptualize their larger settlements as urban and take great pride in them.[1] Indeed, prior to 1975 there were no other communities of comparable size within a 150-mile radius.

As previously stated, until a century ago San Juan Evangelista was a barrio of El Centro. The ties that bind the two separate political entities continue to be very strong, especially in terms of economics and subsistence. Yet some of the old political animosity remains, often finding new causes and occasionally breaking into its more virulent forms—ambushes, vendettas, and mob actions that require the presence of state militia to keep the peace. But for the most part, peace prevails on the surface although the people have long memories.[2]

The central barrios of El Centro constitute the "downtown" section. This is where the market places, city hall and other government offices, the bank, the post office, the telegraph office, public telephones, movie theaters, drugstores, and a

---

[1]An informant who took her teacher training and lived for several years in Oaxaca de Juarez expressed great admiration for El Centro, inquiring if I had not been surprised to find such a great city when I first arrived. Conversely, tourists and residents of Mexican metropolitan areas generally view the Isthmus centers as exceptionally rural and lacking in comforts, either scorning them as impossibly backward and isolated or valuing them for their provincial quaintness.

[2]Several years prior to my fieldwork, the presidente of El Centro was assassinated by members of a political faction whose purported leader was a native son of San Juan Evangelista, although he had not lived in the pueblo for years. Justice being swift in the Isthmus, he was arrested and almost immediately met with some sort of fatal accident. The residents of San Juan were so incensed by the sordid affair that economic sanctions (a beer boycott) were imposed on a prominent member of the opposing faction, a distributor for a major brand of beer. In 1966, trucks bearing that brand name were still prohibited from making deliveries or even entering San Juan Evangelista.

relatively small number of commercial establishments are located. As in all of Latin America, traditionally the commercial center is also the most prestigious place to live, the "high rent" district not only for businesses but for residences as well. Virtually all of the *mestizo* (non-ethnic Mexicans) and other non-Zapotec families, as well as most of the wealthier, more mestisized Zapotecs, live in the central part of El Centro. Around the inevitable central plaza streets are paved and local and long-distance buses and trucks roar around the plaza, exhaust pipes unhampered by mufflers, 24 hours a day.[3] In this small area around the central plaza all the exciting contacts with the outside world take place. Weary, overheated tourists detour the block off the Inter-American Highway to buy a cold drink or mail a letter, rest briefly, and then flit away down the highway, but not before at least one woman from San Jacinto has tried to sell them a "silk" hammock or a girl from San Juan Evangelista has pushed her *totopos* (oven-baked tortillas) under their noses with such persistence that they purchased a few in self-defense. The quadrangle is also the nerve center of all of El Centro, San Juan Evangelista, and the surrounding hinterland. News and gossip radiates out from here to the barrios and San Juan in a surprisingly rapid and efficient manner, and local news trickles into the center and spreads outward along similar routes, carried by women going to and from market and employees returning from jobs.

The six or so outlying barrios of El Centro lack most of the "urban" character of the center and differ little from San Juan Evangelista. The streets are unsurfaced, on the perimeters usually unlighted; *agua potable* (drinkable water) from the district purifying plant may be lacking entirely or available only at a communal outlet; electricity may be lacking in *solares* (house compounds) or consist of no more than a bare bulb. The farther from the center, the less likelihood that a given household will have "modern" plumbing (locally defined as a flush toilet, water piped into a shower, and some sort of drainage system), although households on the hillsides rather close to the center also have mostly primitive sanitary facilities due to the cost of piping water uphill. A number of houses in the outlying barrios have dirt floors, and some, especially around the perimeters, are no more than *chozas* (crude huts), with reed walls chinked with mud, thatched roofs, and dirt floors. During the dry season the flat sandy river bottom often attracts large numbers of squatters from elsewhere who build shelters from reeds, paper cartons, and whatever else they can find. When water released from the dam fills the river banks during the rainy season the squatters must seek other shelter or be washed away. The El Centro police force the people to move on from time to time, but others soon replace them.

On the whole, however, most Zapotec dwellings are of *material,* meaning locally made but relatively costly adobe or concrete blocks for walls, tiles for roofing, and often, cement floors. A house of material is highly valued as a status symbol, as a sign of being "civilized." Many families reside in chozas near their fields part of the time, and these small native structures seemed to me to be quite comfortable and well suited to the climate as well as cheap and easy to erect.

[3]Streets around the central plaza were paved about 1964. Before that, they were cobblestone. But even the paved streets are frequently covered with several inches of mud washed down from the hillsides during rainstorms. By 1990 most of the streets of the central barrios of El Centro were paved and buses and trucks had been banished from the central market area to a newer bus terminal on the outskirts of the city.

Street in Lower San Juan (1982)

Inhabitants of some of the outlying barrios are more isolated from the central district than are the Juanecos, having to walk the two or more miles to and from the center when they lack bus fare or during hours when buses do not run. Taxis are available in the center but are infrequent and difficult to snag in the outlying areas. There are few private telephones, almost all belonging to businesses or professionals.

Residents of the central district of El Centro consider themselves socially superior to persons in the outlying areas. Generally speaking they are apt to have a higher standard of living and a better education and income and often are outsiders, but even a poor Zapotec widow who happens to live in the central area because three generations of her family have occupied her modest house will feel herself to be more civilized simply by the location of the dwelling. Mestizos and other outsiders who live in the center look down on the rest of the population as *sin cultura* (lacking in culture). As a native of Mexico City, whose family owns a business in El Centro, explained:

> Most people here don't know how to live in a civilized way. That's why we call them "sin cultura." They don't know how to enjoy life, just throw their money away on beer-drinking and fiestas. A trip to Veracruz or Tuxtla to them would be a big adventure. Some people have quite a bit of wealth but they don't have culture and they are too ignorant to enjoy the wealth they have. They live in the old way, invest in gold jewelry, spend time and money giving and attending fiestas, probably live in a house with no floors or plumbing, throw their garbage into the center of the solar, and allow the pigs and chickens to run all over the solar. They live on *pozol* (corn gruel) and tortillas with a little salt shrimp and dry cheese and think that's the life. And the chances are good that they can't even write their own name.

Thus traditional Zapotec peasant culture is scorned by the majority of local elites, although the latter would be mostly middle-class in more urban settings. The Juanecos bear the heaviest burden of this attitude because they are the largest concentration of the most traditional peasant population in the immediate vicinity.

From the central district of El Centro, no sign directs the visitor to San Juan and few strangers are aware that a pueblo of more than 6,000 people lies just behind the mountain, not more than a twenty-minute walk from the center of one pueblo to the center of the other. The only clues to San Juan's existence are the signs on the rickety, lumbering *urbanos* (urban buses)—El Segundo, Santa Inez, San Juan, and other outlying destinations including *el panteon* (cemetery). The buses come in, fill up, and leave the central district continuously during daylight hours. The bus to San Juan runs at half-hour intervals and, like all the others, is laden with women and girls, mostly in native dress, going home with baskets, bundles, and net bags filled with daily purchases of foodstuffs, sometimes including a brace of live iguanas bound and gagged, a hobbled hen, or a live turkey. Usually the driver and the fare collector are the only men aboard.[4] The urbano gets under way with effort, creaking and groaning over the rough and narrow streets as it works its way toward San Juan, a gigantic metal version of the *criollo* (local breed) sows that root in the same path. At what appears to be the end of the street on the river bluff, the bus makes a 90-degree turn uphill, squeezes through a narrow passage hewn in solid rock, and emerges into San Juan Evangelista.

SAN JUAN EVANGELISTA, THE PUEBLO

The church dominates the visitor's first impression of San Juan. Standing just inside the entrance to the pueblo, it faces the entrance passageway rather than the center of San Juan, giving an impression of having turned its back on the pueblo, a stance perhaps symbolic of a mutual indifference between the citizens and the official Church. Still, the church structure is more attractive and in better repair than any in El Centro, for while there is general distrust and suspicion of the clergy, there is also great respect for the saints and a considerable degree of religious activity and piety in day-to-day living. Juanecos practice their folk Catholicism rather independently as they have for generations, sometimes to the amazement and distress of visiting *padres* (priests).[5]

Although the usual practice has been to hire a priest from El Centro when needed, in 1966 a few prominent citizens of San Juan had succeeded in securing a resident priest and two nuns who had begun a parochial school for boys in the church compound. The young priest was forced to leave after a few months because of ill health. The two women stayed on for a time, but even the little confidence

---

[4]For the most part, men who have business in outlying areas hire a taxi, while resident men are away from the pueblos during daylight hours, most often working in their fields. The campesino who happens to be in El Centro during daylight hours will probably choose to walk home, saving the 30-centavo fare and leaving more space on the bus for the women and their ever-present bundles and baskets of food. As a rule Zapotec men do nòt carry burdens.

[5]This is a pattern typical of many Mesoamerican peasant communities.

Commuting by Moto (1990)

they had gained in the people of San Juan eventually flickered and died, and they too left.[6]

About three blocks beyond the church lies the central *parque* (town plaza), appropriately modest for a former barrio of El Centro, bordered on three sides by streets and on the fourth by the small public market place combined with the town's government offices. In 1966 the upper grades of elementary school and municipal buildings, including the jail, occupied one side of the square. By 1990 all had been moved to other sites. A block beyond the central plaza stands the modest and ancient church of San Bartolo Xadani, still in use but bearing the marks of its age. Long ago it marked the focal point of a barrio by the same name.

There is no business district as such in San Juan, a reflection of its past history as barrio and its continuing dependence on El Centro. Five or six general stores, located in the front part or lower floor of the owner's dwelling, are scattered over the pueblo. There are several *nixtamal* (corn-grinding) mills, each serving its particular neighborhood, and a variety of workshops of tailors, sandal makers, carpenters, jewelers, seamstresses, and the like, as well as the inevitable rash of *cantinas* (bars), and *tienditas* (tiny stores), all operated from the proprietors' residences. San Juan has no postoffice, no telegraph office, no drugstore, and only one medical doctor, relying on El Centro to

---

[6]The two nuns were rather young and certainly unprepared for life in a rural peasant community. When a *borracho* (drunk) stumbled to their door one night and begged for sexual favors, they were properly outraged but genuinely perplexed by such barbarous audacity.

fulfill such needs.[7] In these ways San Juan is as dependent as any outlying barrio of El Centro. But in the minds of Juanecos there is one enormous difference between the status of San Juan and the barrios.

That difference is political independence, and the residents of San Juan Evangelista cherish it intensely. Repeatedly, informants' comments included: "San Juan es un pueblo libre." And, contrary to fact, most people will argue that this is a special political status accorded to very few pueblos in the entire nation. This special status they owe to their hero, Porfirio Diaz.

The pueblo of San Juan Evangelista had a population of approximately 6,300 in 1967. In 1990 I estimate the number of inhabitants has more than doubled. A few thousand others live in the municipio in the several unincorporated rancheros. Some families have permanent dwellings in San Juan Evangelista and another house, often a choza, near their fields with various members of the family alternating between the two as work and business dictate. A sample of 210 households reveals a median household size of 5.6 persons. In 1967 there were around 1,100 households in San Juan; in 1990 there are well over double that number.

Isthmus Zapotecs favor virilocal residence (that is, the newlyweds live with the husband's family after marriage), but lineally extended families of the sample households were equally divided between virilocal and uxorilocal residence (couple resides with wife's parents after marriage). Other things being equal, the virilocal pattern is followed; but if the bride is an only daughter, the bride's parents are considerably more prosperous than the groom's, the groom is an orphan, or the virilocal household is crowded, the young couple may find living with the wife's parents more convenient. Today, most young couples express a desire to establish their own household immediately upon marriage and a few manage to do so. Most find it economically impossible for a few years at least.

Most residents of San Juan were born in the pueblo and have never lived elsewhere. Only 5 of 119 household heads were not natives, and all but one of these were born in nearby municipios. A significant number of young men between the ages of fifteen and thirty-five are absent from the pueblo. They leave to seek better job opportunities elsewhere and to attend school. They return intermittently and keep in contact with their kin, but the same forces that cause them to leave usually prevent their returning permanently to San Juan. This emigration pattern, of long duration, has serious consequences not only for the marriageable girls left behind but also for the pueblo as a whole since the more ambitious, enterprising, better educated, and perhaps more intelligent young men of each generation, who might otherwise have made the greatest contributions to their home community, are forced by economic circumstances to leave. The other side of the emigration coin benefits the pueblo, for emigrant Zapotecs tend to remain emotionally attached to the place of their birth, maintaining extensive kin ties, and returning for public and family fiestas whenever possible. Often migrants send money to parents and siblings, and not infrequently children of siblings and even cousins live for years with their city

---

[7]Efforts were being made in 1968 to secure a telegraph office in San Juan. In 1969 a public telephone was installed in one of the tiendas, only to be taken out a short time later while the building underwent major alterations. In 1990 there is a post office, a telegraph office, and many other improvements—as discussed in Chapter 10.

kinfolk in order to benefit from the better educational opportunities in city schools. Favored migration destinations are Mexico City, Veracruz, and the cities on the Gulf coast of the geographical Isthmus—the latter attractive because of proximity and job opportunities in the petroleum industries. At least two "colonias" of Mexico City are heavily populated with Isthmus Zapotecs.

Traditionally, Zapotec has been the first language of all Isthmus Zapotecs and one of the most important means of maintaining their ethnicity, but it has also been a deterrent to integration and opportunity in the national culture. Formerly, children learned the national language only when they attended school, and many children did not attend regularly enough. Nowadays many parents recognize that the key to improving one's economic and social status in the national culture is a command of the national language. A few more progressive parents who speak fluent Spanish try to teach their children only Spanish. This is more apparent in other communities, however. In San Juan Evangelista less than 4 percent of the population speaks only the national language, and 96 percent speaks Zapotec, 43 percent monolingually (VIII Censo General).[8] In San Juan, with the highest incidence of retention of the indigenous language of any Zapotec community in the Isthmus, one seldom hears the national language except in schools, on official occasions, and when residents are speaking to outsiders. Even the announcements made over the public address system are mostly in Zapotec.

By contrast, more than 60 percent of the inhabitants of El Centro speak only Spanish. According to the 1960 census, 28 percent of the residents of San Juan age thirteen and over were literate, but if the test of literacy were comprehension of a first-grade reader instead of the word of the individual, 10 percent literacy might be a generous figure. Formal schooling is not stressed for girls, and this is reflected in literacy statistics which indicate that twice as many men as women are literate.

There are two primary schools in San Juan, one with six grades, the other with only the first three. Until 1967, the only secondary school (comparable to our junior high school) was in El Centro. Beginning in 1967, seventh-grade evening classes were being offered to about 40 young men in San Juan. Shockingly few children graduate from primary school and fewer still continue beyond that level. In 1967, 104 students were continuing their education beyond the sixth grade, less than 9 percent of San Juan's population between the ages of fifteen and twenty-three. It is not always indifference to education that keeps children at home, although this is sometimes a factor. More often families cannot afford to send all their school-age children to classes simultaneously. Boys attend more than girls because education is perceived as more useful to boys and because girls are more useful at home. Although 46 percent of the boys and 31 percent of the girls between the ages of six and fourteen were enrolled in school in 1967, perhaps only about one-third attend classes regularly. Often one or two children are sent to school for a year or so and then they remain at home while one or two others are sent, all ending with a minimal and equally ineffective education. Another method is to educate one son for a profession or white collar job, the whole household pouring resources toward that goal, making great sacrifices to insure the parents against a destitute old age and at the same time elevating the family's social status.

[8]There are many more bilingual speakers in 1990 but a high retention of the Zapotec language. On the streets of the town one still seldom hears Spanish spoken and Zapotec is still the first language of virtually every Zapotec child.

4 / The Subsistence Base

At first European contact, Zapotecs were already accomplished cultivators, sharing with other Mesoamericans the long history of New World plant domestication. In the Isthmus, people were growing corn, varieties of squash and chiles, cotton, and a wide variety of other vegetables and tropical fruits. One of the fruits, the zapote, was so prevalent in the entire Zapotec area that the Spaniards referred to the people by the name of the fruit.[1]

Irrigation was essential in many places and was practiced wherever their paleotechnology made it possible. Isthmus Zapotecs were fortunate in the abundant supply of fish and shrimp readily available in the great saltwater lagoons, the sea, rivers, and fresh water lagoons. Sometime in the distant past the people discovered how to preserve these products by salting and drying them in the sun. The Gulf of Tehuantepec, near the shores at least, has a high salt content. Perhaps centuries before the Contact people built earthen salt pans at the edges of the saline lagoons which could be filled with salt water and then allowed to drain, leaving only the dry salt crystals. Salted fish and shrimp are still the main sources of whole protein in the native diet, and the salt pans of the coastal lagoons continue to be a major source of salt for the entire republic.

The Spaniards introduced many new cultigens, useful domestic animals, and a new technology based on beasts of burden which set in motion changes in subsistence techniques all over Mesoamerica. While many European cultigens were not suited to the Isthmus climate, chickens, burros, horses, cattle, sheep, goats, and oxen, along with oxcarts and the primitive Mediterranean plow, revolutionized agriculture. Still today, for the majority of Zapotec campesinos, oxen, oxcarts, and the Mediterranean plows are as essential as they have been for the past four centuries.

Zapotecs practice mixed cash–subsistence farming, raising some crops totally for sale and others mostly for home consumption. Older informants in San Juan remember when sugar cane was the principal cash crop and quite a profitable one for a time in the early quarter of this century. Then prices fell on the international market to very low levels and canefields were gradually converted to other more profitable crops. The triad of bananas, mangoes, and coconut palms became popular in irrigated, wind-protected fields and continues to be important although

[1]Zapotecs call themsevles *za*, "the people," when they have occasion to distinguish themselves as an ethnic group, which is rare. In practice they follow the widespread Mesoamerican custom of identifying themselves and others by the pueblo of birth and by region rather than by ethnic or linguistic criteria. A native of San Juan is a Juaneco, a native of the Isthmus is an Istmeno. Thus, a resident of San Juan will be referred to regionally as a Juaneco and as an Istmeno when outside the region.

Men Harvesting Sesame (1975)

not certainly very profitable. The pattern is to plant bananas in the plot and mangoes and coconuts around the perimeter. Mangoes, which become very large, dense trees, offer additional wind protection to the delicate banana plants while the tall, slender coconut palms can be planted between the mango trees, producing coconuts without taking additional space.

Recent introductions include sesame and sorghum, both totally cash crops, but the ancient maize remains the great crop favorite because of its versatility (cash or subsistence), its familiarity, and its vast importance in native diet. Government agronomists are encouraging the cultivation on a larger scale of some long established crops such as tomatoes, sweet potatotes, and native flowers in an effort to increase cash income sources.[2]

Land Tenure and the Social System

The social system is conceptualized as a great network of interrelationships and interdependencies. A shift in one part, perhaps a change so small it is unnoticed by

[2]Actually a great many common vegetables and fruits are not suited to the Isthmus climate. These include such staples as beans and onions and such familiar and mundane vegetables as white potatoes. All of these must be imported from higher elevations. Beans and onions are the only imports that are regular items in native diet. White potatoes are a luxury food. Even hybrid maize varieties have proved difficult to grow under local conditions. Although experimentations by government agronomists continue, most campesinos still plant the old inbred criollo maize.

the people themselves, may eventually engender unanticipated and important changes in other parts of the social system. One of the most obvious areas where changes begin is the subsistence base—crops, technology, and amount of arable land per family, for example. In agrarian social systems the total amount of land available, its distribution patterns, and the types of land tenure are so important to understanding the total social system that they are among the first subjects the fieldworker hopes to broach. In San Juan Evangelista, land is a very delicate subject. Direct questions by outsiders will be met with evasions, fabrications, or simply silence because Juanecos find themselves in an enviable but insecure position regarding the very core of their existence, land.

Basically there are two types of land tenure in the Isthmus: private and communal. Private property, most familiar to us, includes the right of the individual to sell the land. Communal property, on the other hand, does not include this right but only the right of the individual to use the land for a certain period of time. The title to the land remains with the community. San Juan Evangelista is unique among the Isthmus municipios in that its communal land dates from its separation from El Centro in 1868 at which time several thousand *hectares* of land were granted the new municipio. Other communal land tenure dates from the years after the Mexican Revolution (1910–1920) when the national government redistributed large holdings to groups of campesinos who formed *ejidos*. There is some ejidal land in the Isthmus, but private tenure is the more valued type. Thus, San Juan is unique not only in its long history of communal tenure but also in the large amount of its total land area that remains in communal as opposed to private tenure (80 and 20 percent respectively).

In 1868 nobody worried much about precise municipio boundaries. Most of the land was marginal, supporting spinous scrub forest, and used mainly for gathering wild plant foods, a little hunting, firewood, and making charcoal. It would support some livestock during most of the year, but animals usually had to be fed supplementally toward the end of the long dry season. Certain parts of this el monte could be farmed by slash-and-burn techniques, but this method produced a poor crop for the amount of work involved and never was favored.[3] In spite of the poor quality of much of this land, the people of San Juan looked upon their communal lands as a vast untapped reservoir of resources. Many Zapotec campesinos in surrounding municipios had become alienated from the land over time by means fair and foul, and the message was not lost on the Juanecos. The municipio apparently undertook a program of land acquisition that appears to have continued until recently.

All this communal land makes Juanecos feel especially fortunate compared to their neighbors, but it also generates a high level of anxiety and suspicion, a suspicion that seems to border on paranoia at times. Municipio boundaries, never certain, have suddenly become more critical as population has increased, and at the same time the possibility of reclamation of much of the land through extensive irrigation has recently become a reality. Anthropologists have postulated a close

---

[3]Slash-and-burn cultivation involves cutting, drying, and burning the native ground cover (here scrub trees and thorny bushes) and planting the crop in the ashes. Where employed, the method usually entails opening new plots after a few seasons and abandoning the old ones as they become less productive, a system which requires a great deal of land.

relationship between encysted or closed peasant communities and communal land tenure.[4] Although San Juan is not completely encysted, it is certainly the most conservative, self-protective municipio in the region by a number of criteria including retention of native language, anxiety and suspicion toward outsiders, and Juanecos' reputation in El Centro as *muy cerrados* (closed). Almost certainly, anxiety over land has increased since the initiation of the regional irrigation project in 1964. Juanecos have tried, more or less successfully, to keep government surveyors off their land, the municipio is embroiled in several lawsuits over boundaries, and open discussions of land with or before outsiders are discouraged.

Paradoxically, communal tenure has worked to pull the community together against the outside world, and at the same time, it has worked to create internal dissension and factionalism. Some progressives feel that the municipio is "land poor." They urge that some of the land be sold to neighboring municipios who are creating problems about boundaries and that the money be used for desperately needed capital improvements such as roads, land leveling, auxiliary canals, and other projects. The conservatives consider this a sell-out and from bitter past experience believe the money would disappear into politicians' pockets and result in little or no public good.

Communal tenure does not necessitate the working of land cooperatively. In San Juan, families are allotted individual plots of land which they then farm independently just as they do private property. The communal plots are to revert to the community after two years of non-use or at the death of the original applicant, but probably neither of these rules has ever been enforced. Many households in San Juan still farm communal land which their parents or grandparents were allotted, often unaware that it is not their private property until they try to sell it. Communal land can be converted to private property by paying a prescribed amount ($750 per hectare in 1967).[5] Such converted land cannot be sold by the original owner for more than the conversion price plus improvements. Heirs of the original owner may sell the land at market price. About 20 percent of San Juan's land is privately owned (1967), including virtually all of the choice irrigated and wind-protected fields fanning out from the edge of the pueblo for an average of 3 miles. These *terrenos de labor* (garden plots) are favored for bananas, mangoes, coconuts, and other fruits, but a considerable number of plots are also planted to maize and some also to sesame.

With an abundance of land and communal tenure, one might assume that every household would have some land, but this is not the case. Sixteen percent of a small sample of forty-four households reported that they did not farm, either because there

---

[4]Wolf defines as closed peasant communities those which "restrict their membership, maintain a religious system, enforce mechanisms which ensure the redistribution or destruction of surplus wealth, and uphold barriers against the entry of goods and ideas produced outside the community" as opposed to the open peasant community where communal jurisdiction over land is absent, membership is unrestricted, and wealth is not redistributed" (Wolf 1967, p. 235). San Juan Evangelista is not a complete closed peasant community, yet it possesses in varying degrees a number of the characteristics of a closed community.

[5]All monetary values are given in Mexican pesos throughout the monograph unless otherwise stated. At the time of fieldwork, 1966–1967, the rate of exchange was approximately 12.5 pesos to one U.S. dollar. In 1990 it was just under 3000 pesos to the dollar. Unless otherwise noted, the 1967 exchange rate is used throughout.

was no able-bodied man in the household or the men of the household had full-time occupations, which left no time for farming—occupations such as pottery-making, carpentry, and teaching. Farming, however, is the main occupation of the majority of men in San Juan Evangelista, and perhaps 90 percent of the households gain part of their income from agriculture.

Other Property and Ownership Rights

In addition to the fields held in private ownership, the most important items of property include solares, household equipment, animals, farm equipment, clothing, and jewelry. Sons normally inherit the solar of the parents while daughters are expected to move to the husband's solar at marriage. But daughters always have the right to return to their natal solar to live if they are widowed, and they have the right to remain in the solar all their lives if they do not marry, brothers supporting them if necessary. If there are two or more sons and the solar is large, it may be partitioned off as each son marries and eventually split into several small solares. Fields, when privately owned, are inherited bilaterally, although sons seem to inherit the best and largest fields. All tools, oxcarts, and other farming implements belong to men, as do the larger domestic animals. Oxen, tools, and equipment are usually inherited by sons, but herds of cattle and goats are divided more or less equally among all the children. Household furnishings are simple and few and invariably are considered a part of the solar when an estate is settled. At marriage, the daughters have already received dowries, consisting of a *baul* (wooden trunk on legs) containing clothing and a variable amount of gold coin jewelry, depending on the family's resources. The jewelry belongs to the wife and is normally inherited by daughters, although no heirloom value is attached to it. Because jewelry functions primarily as a form of investment and collateral, it is rare for the same pieces to be passed on from mother to daughters through more than one generation, rare even for a mother still to possess the jewelry from her dowry when her daughters marry. Jewelry is owned by women, but is pawned or sold for the benefit of the household just as land is, although much more frequently. The order of preference for raising cash to meet an emergency is generally: Selling pigs, selling cattle other than oxen, pawning jewelry, selling jewelry, selling oxen, pawning land, and selling land. Since many households do not own cattle and some do not own pigs, pawning jewelry is the most frequent first choice, with jewelry selling close behind. Pawned or sold jewelry will be retrieved or replaced as soon as finances permit. There is a great deal of trade and pawning of gold jewelry, much of which is carried on by women, but most of the large money-lending operations are run by men. The government pawnshop in El Centro, which averages 800 transactions per month, represents a very small part of the total volume of transactions because most persons prefer the more liberal terms and higher interest rates of private lenders.

Except for earrings and an occasional modest necklace, women wear gold jewelry only at fiestas where the more prosperous may literally be laden with heavy coin collars and necklaces, elaborate earrings, and perhaps two or three rings on each finger of both hands. But one does not have to be wealthy to wear embroidered fiesta costumes and gold jewelry to fiestas. Both can be borrowed or rented for a nominal fee, although that is usually the resort only of visiting outsiders and an occasional wily maiden hoping to snare a novio.

Men, with some exceptions to be discussed later, do not wear jewelry, but a man without sisters may inherit it, and if the man is going to pawn jewelry for masculine purposes such as buying seed corn, either he or the wife may carry the jewelry to the money-lender.

The Sexual Division of Labor

All human societies observe certain rules when it comes to what tasks are considered appropriate for each sex, although the rules vary from one society to the next. Division of labor by sex seems to be an efficient way to carry out everyday functions of households even in industrialized societies such as our own where the household is mainly only a consuming (as opposed to producing) unit. In peasant and tribal societies where the household may be both, the division of labor by sex is generally rather strictly prescribed.

In San Juan the household is the basic production unit as well as the basic consumption unit. Paleotechnic farming, while it is the main occupation of the majority of male household heads, is not a lucrative venture under the best of conditions because of its high labor requirements, risk of crop failures, and low productivity. As a result, households diversify. The more occupations and skills members of a household command, the more secure is the household against economic disaster. All productive members of the household are expected to have one or more means of bringing in money. Very often an individual learns several skills that he practices parttime in addition to his regular occupation. A man who considers his major occupation farming (which includes the care of large animals such as oxen, cattle, horses, and goats) may also be a barber in the evenings and perhaps make fireworks in his spare time.

Most wives state that their principal occupation is "housewife," a term which includes a variety of economic functions not normally included in the term in English. For example, virtually every adult woman in San Juan can prepare tortillas and some other food for sale if the need arises. It is a rare household that does not include at least one woman who regularly processes and sells something. The vast majority of women do so intermittently at least, but even if selling is a regular activity, it is almost never considered an occupation.

The list of women's occupations in Table 4.1 is the author's construct in that women *always* gave homemaking as their principal occupation, their income-producing activities being considered a normal part of homemaking. Principal occupations were elicited by rephrasing the question along lines of what they usually did to produce income and how much time they spent at such activities. From a comparison of men's and women's principal occupations, several things are apparent. First, no women are employed for wages—jobs that are rare and highly prized because any type of regular income, no matter how little, is thought to be economically advantageous compared to self-employment. Women normally do not acquire the skills for wage and salary work. If they do, as in the case of the school teacher, they may not find a position because competition from men will be keen.

TABLE 4.1   PRINCIPAL OCCUPATIONS OF SAMPLE HOUSEHOLD
HEADS BY SEX

Men (N = 194)		Women (N = 174)	
Occupation	Nos.	Occupation	Nos.
Agriculture		Producer–Vendor	
Campesino	115	Tortillera–Totopera	68
Day Laborer	1	Baker	9
Dairyman	1	Seamstress	7
Crafts		Revendor	
Tailor	8	Tiendita Operator	11
Jeweler	7	Revendor in Market	10
Musician	6	Traveling Revendors	7
Carpenter	6	Comerciante	4
Potter	5	Cantina Operator	2
Mason	4		
Barber	3	Other	
Butcher	3	Housewife	41
Baker	1	School Teacher	1
Radio Repairman	1	Practical Nurse	1
Oxcart Repairman	1	Masseuse	1
Employees			
Clerical Worker	8		
School Teacher	3		
Wage Worker	2		
Truck Driver	1		
Soldier	1		
Mechanic	1		
Tradesmen			
Comerciante	7		
Traveling Revendor*	1		
Cantina Operator	1		
Other			
Masseur	1		

*Native of Oaxaca de Juarez.

Second, of twenty-six male occupations and fourteen female occupations, only eight are filled by both sexes. Of these, seamstress–tailor and masseur–masseuse are sex-specific (tailors make men's clothing, and seamstresses make women's clothing), and the four women *comerciantes* (businesswomen) and the one male traveling revendor all represent half of husband–wife teams. The only listed occupations considered equally suitable for either sex are baker and potter. But even in pottery-making women usually specialize in small items, and men in large, heavy ones. Third, a difference that is not apparent in Table 4.1 relates to time spent practicing a principal occupation. Relatviely few women devote what would be considered fulltime by male standards to their principal occupation. This is not surprising since women's income-producing principal occupations compete with a number of other household duties, many of which take precedence over producing income.

Processing and Selling

The traditional and still prevalent basic division of labor between the sexes in San Juan Evangelista is simply this: Men are the producers and women are the processors and vendors of the men's production. This basic theme is expanded and adjusted to meet the individual needs of the particular household. The processing–vending role of women is extremely important to the economic success of the household—equally as important as the producer role of the men, as will become apparent. The most common processing–vending operation (and probably one of the least profitable because of competition and market limitations) is making tortillas and totopos for sale from maize produced by the household. Every adult woman possesses the necessary skills, and most make tortillas for their own household at least part of the time.[6] Since it is a time-consuming job, the woman may prefer to buy tortillas from a neighbor daily or occasionally. The middle-class mestizo population of El Centro offers another outlet because tortillas are usually not made at home unless there are servants to do it.

If a Juaneca makes tortillas all day, which she rarely does, she can earn from $8 to $10, which compares favorably with what a man can earn by working for wages in the fields. Both jobs are of equally low prestige because neither is thought to require any special skills and neither produces enough income for the daily needs of even the smallest household. More often a young woman tied to her household by small children earns a few extra *pesos* by making only enough extra tortillas for a neighbor or two.

The making of totopos is more involved, requiring an oven which all households do not have, at least $3 of scarce firewood, and the undivided attention of the totopera from start to finish. Thus, making totopos takes on some of the aspects of a specialization. Since it is a day-long job (once the oven is heated the totopos must be baked three or four at a time without pause) and one not amenable to interruptions, it is often taught to teenage daughters. Because of the keeping qualities of totopos, which tortillas lack, there is always a ready market. Many are exported to other parts of the republic. With the same amount of nixtamal as required for tortillas, a woman can net between $10 and $16 per day making totopos. It is a dreaded task, however, because the totopera must lean over the open barrel-shaped oven and place her entire lower arm inside to paste the raw totopo on the oven wall, repeating the motion to remove it after baking. Thus she must stand over the hot oven for hours, inserting her bare arm every minute or two. Women who regularly make totopos are said to bear the marks of their occupation in badly scarred hands and arms from the inevitable burns. It is rumored that if one pursues the occupation too many years she will lose her eyesight from the toxic effects of heat and smoke. Often the young totopera is persuaded to keep at her task only because she is allowed to take the totopos to sell on the streets of El Centro in the later afternoon, a reward as valued by San Juan girls as allowing a sixteen-year-old to take the family car in our culture.

There are numerous types of processing and selling, many of them requiring the

---

[6]Sixty-eight percent of the sample households made tortillas for their own household use almost daily.

Woman Making Totopos (1982)

purchase of some or all of the raw materials. Some common activities are: selling sliced cucumbers, pineapples, oranges and other "snack" foods to passersby in front of one's house; buying fish and shrimp from coastal people, salting and drying them in one's solar, and selling them locally or in urban markets; buying sugar and *cacao* (cocoa) beans and preparing chocolate tablets for sale; buying sea turtle eggs in season, boiling and selling them immediately or drying them to sell later;[7] making drinks of crushed fruit, water, and sugar and selling the beverage by the glass to passersby; and preparing a great variety of cooked foods for sale in the market places or on the streets.

There are also a great many things which can simply be bought in bulk and sold in very small quantities at higher prices because most households operate on a minimal cash basis, buying only enough of an item for immediate needs.[8] Some households also produce a number of things which can be sold without processing—for example, bananas, mangoes, and maize. A prestigious business venture, but one which seems to earn little if anything, is the tiendita, often no more than a shelf just inside the house entrance stocked with a few staple items for sale. Common items include such durables as soap, brooms, matches, beans, cigarettes, and candles. If the tiendita is near one of the schools perhaps a few inexpensive notebooks and pencils, hard candy, and chewing gum will comprise the inventory. Whether or not one actually nets any income, there are advantages in having a tiendita in one's house. The family can draw on its stock, which is purchased "wholesale," and the mere fact of the tiendita's presence adds to the family's social status. Although the possibility seems never to be realized, people believe that the tiendita may lead them into becoming a big comerciante some day.[9] The husband, brother, or son may provide the initial small capital outlay to begin a tiendita, but wives, mothers, grandmothers, or maiden aunts invariably operate them. How many tienditas are in operation at any one time is difficult to determine. They come into existence and disappear as Arabian sheiks fold their tents and steal away in the night. Perhaps about 10 percent of the total households operate stores ranging in size from the smallest tiendita to the largest commercial enterprise in the pueblo, with most falling in the small range.

The admired comerciante is a man engaged in several different business enterprises of which the comparatively large, well-stocked tienda is usually one. While his wife tends the store, perhaps he also runs a cantina, owns or rents several farms operated with hired labor, almost surely lends money on land and jewelry, and probably acts as a buyer of local crops (maize, mangoes, bananas, and such) either on commission for a city wholesaler or on his own. Although the entire household is involved, often including one or more married sons and their wives, the elder male household head is considered the comerciante.

Selling by Men

As stated earlier, basically men produce and women process and sell, but there are certain exceptions. When maize is sold unshelled directly after harvest, the man usually seeks a buyer, perhaps a local comerciante, and delivers the maize to him by the *carreta* (oxcart). The same is true of mangoes if they must be sold locally to a

---

[7]Illegal since the mid-1970s because the turtle is endangered.
[8]This is due in part to the lack of means of preserving perishable foods in a tropical climate, but it also applies to such staples as soap powder, sugar, rice, and beans. For example, a woman preparing to wash clothes buys just enough soap to do the amount of laundry at hand. Part of this is due to economic necessity and part is simply habit.
[9]Of the four or five most successful comerciantes in San Juan, none began with a tiendita.

Morning Street Market (1975)

wholesaler, and men also sell large animals, whose care and maintenance is also their responsibility. Craftsmen often sell their own products, either from the shop or by delivering them to customers, but some men (for example, potters) concentrate on their craft and let their wives handle the selling. Comparing men's and women's selling, one finds a clear difference in quantities, types of sales, and context of negotiations. Men sell large quantities of those products that can be sold immediately after harvest; sales are usually made by men to a wholesaler (except in the case of animals); and the context of the sales negotiations will not be the market place. Women sell in essentially three contexts: the home, the streets, and the market places. Men sometimes conclude a sale agreement in the home but never sell in the streets or in the market places.[10]

Selling by Women

The market places are overwhelmingly a woman's milieu. In addition to more than 350 permanent vendors who pay a fee to the municipal government for their space in El Centro market, there are anywhere from 200 to perhaps 1,000 ambulantes per day, women who have no permanent space but squat or stand in the aisles or move around through the market structure and adjacent streets selling their wares. Most of these women sell products of their household, and the quantities

---

[10]Approximately 10 percent of the more than 350 permanent vendors in the El Centro market places are men, almost all non-Zapotecs. Two or three Zapotec men have become owners of puestos by inheritance. In one case, an adult son who had helped his mother since childhood, gradually took over the entire operation until his mother more or less retired. In another case, the man had been hired as an orphan boy to help in the puesto of a mestizo. He inherited the business when the old man died.

sold in any one day are usually quite small. One area of one of the market places is designated as a wholesale area. Here women will sell local products either in bulk or in lots as small as a half dozen items, the larger the purchase the lower the unit price. Truckloads of imported fruits such as oranges and pineapples are sold in this same type of graduated wholesale–retail price structure that allows many Zapotec revendors to buy a dozen or two fruits and make a few pesos by reselling them by the slice.[11] A woman may sell every day for a week or so seasonally, once or twice a week as when she has enough ripe bananas to make the effort worthwhile, or a couple of hours a day at a particular time, as when she sells tortillas or prepared foods. The pattern of her market selling will be conditioned by the products she sells.

In the market places the customers, too, are almost all women. The market places, in fact, are the supermarkets of the Isthmus, the only place fresh fruits and vegetables, fresh meat, fish, and poultry can be purchased and the most convenient place to purchase all sorts of staples, notions, hardware, clothing, and yard goods, as well as a wide variety of prepared foods to eat on the spot or carry out. The several small grocery stores outside the market place in El Centro sell *ultramarinos* (imports) almost exclusively. Their customers are mainly local elites and tourists, the only people who can afford such luxuries. Thus, the entire population depends on the market places for their daily food needs.

During the two or three rush hours (7–10 A.M.) the aisles of the market places are jammed with housewives or their servants purchasing the daily food supply for the household.[12] A popular vendor may make 30 or more sales per hour during the busy period and total as many as 150 sales per day. Sales dwindle after about 11 A.M., and by 2 P.M. the market stalls are deserted. At about 4 P.M. vendors begin arriving to sell to the supper trade, taking up posts on the street outside the market place—where it is cooler. These women are mostly different individuals from the morning vendors. Items for breakfast the following day are also sold at this time. By 8 P.M. this group of vendors has dispersed for the night, but meantime, beginning about 6 P.M., other women have set up portable tables and benches around the central plaza, where they serve meals prepared at home and on their portable charcoal burners. These portable restaurants are in operation until about 10 P.M. on ordinary nights but remain open until 2 or 3 A.M. when there are social events such as fiestas and dances which might bring late customers.

So far we have described only the selling in El Centro. There are also several small plazitas in outlying sections such as the one in San Juan where Juanecas, from ten to thirty at any one time, sell to other Juanecas a small selection of prepared dishes, tortillas, sweet rolls, cheese, tomatoes, onions, and fresh beef. Compared to the central market places (the supermarket), the plazitas are the corner grocery where one goes for last minute or emergency food purchases. Their popularity is greatest between 6 and 8 A.M. when many housewives and children come to make purchases for breakfast.

But Juanecas often go farther afield to sell. Some San Juan products such as

---

[11]Most of this type of revending takes place in front of or near the revendor's home in outlying areas and is often the task of young girls. Some girls from El Centro sell around the central plaza, however.
[12]See footnote 8.

bananas, mangoes, coconuts, and coconut tree seedlings, plus small quantities of many other local fruits, are regularly taken to San Jacinto, the regional trade center, where prices are apt to be higher and sales more brisk than in El Centro.[13] Selling in San Jacinto requires the entire day plus the time and expense involved in the 30-mile bus trip. Usually it is well after dusk when the women, from six to thirty, depending on the season, return from San Jacinto, wearily trudging into San Juan with several empty baskets carried one in the other atop their heads, dirty and exhausted from squatting in the tropical sun all day at the edge of the dusty San Jacinto streets.[14]

Some women are *viajeras,* traveling more or less constantly, perhaps between the coastal villages and Oaxaca de Juarez, buying and selling on both ends of the circuit. Women whose households raise mangoes often take these fruits to Oaxaca de Juarez periodically during the two-month mango season, at least doubling their net profit compared to selling them locally on a glutted market. This is wholesale selling in large quantities but it is always done by women. Once the fruits are harvested and delivered to the solar (and harvesting of fruits often involves the whole family), they become the wife's responsibility. She must hire local transport to El Centro and then find and bargain with a *fletero* (truck driver) to haul them to Oaxaca.[15] A woman may have twelve or more baskets of mangoes, each weighing about 200 pounds, in a single shipment. Once shipment is arranged by truck, the Juaneca travels by second-class bus in order to arrive in the city ahead of the mangoes. The fletero will deliver the mangoes to a particular street where mangoes are sold wholesale. Most of the vendors at this time of year will also be women from the Isthmus since this is mango season there but not elsewhere. Several vendors will probably be from San Juan. Depending on the number of baskets she has, the Juaneca may sell all the mangoes the first day and return home on the night bus, or she may have to stay over two or even three days, in which case she pays a peso for a sleeping space in the patio of a private residence on the same street. It is a rare Juaneca who ventures out of the immediate vicinity of the market place when she sells in Oaxaca. More often she does not leave the particular street where her product is sold. For example, one informant, Lucia, had been bringing mangoes to the Oaxaca market for the past six or seven seasons, making from six to eight trips each season. A woman of exceptional intelligence and curiosity about the world, she visited the central part of the city for the first time with me, although it is only a distance of about three blocks from the street where she sells.

The reasons women confine themselves to the Oaxaca market place are many. Primarily, the object of the trip is to sell the mangoes and return home as rapidly as possible in order to arrange shipment for the successive picking. Second, the vendor cannot leave her mangoes unattended except for brief periods when a neighbor will sell for her. And further, there is really very little incentive to leave the market area

[13]Prices are higher in San Jacinto because many of San Juan products are difficult to grow around the drier, windier San Jacinto area. Sales are more brisk because this is the main regional trade center, drawing customers from a wide area of the mountains and coast.

[14]San Jacinto practices a type of local protectionism by reserving all shaded places for local vendors. Outsiders, including Juanecas, are assigned space at the edge of the streets outside the market structure where they are forbidden to erect shades. The place where Juanecas sell is in full sun until about 2 P.M. most of the year.

[15]During mangoe season it may take a woman two or three days to locate a fletero with space for her cargo since there is a great demand for fleteros at this time.

Zapotec Viajeras Trading in Huave Village (1975)

since everything a woman may wish to buy is available in the market place and at lower prices than elsewhere in the city. Lucia had always wanted to see the cathedral but feared she would lose her way, being unable to read the street signs and doubtful about her ability to communicate in Spanish. Other informants sometimes stated that they felt conspicuous away from the market places in their traditional clothing when they traveled outside of el Istmo.

Economic Spheres Open Only to Women

By investing time and labor in processing and selling the household production in small quantities, Isthmus Zapotec women are in a position to maximize the household income from that production. The more woman-hours a household can channel into processing and vending, the larger the household income. Extra woman-hours can always be shifted into processing and vending, even lacking production, simply by purchasing the raw products. Extra able-bodied adult women are probably always economically advantageous to the household while extra adult able-bodied men may or may not be, depending upon how much of their time is devoted to some activity which produces income. Men probably produce more income per man-hour than women when they are employed, but tend to be underemployed compared to women. That is, men have more leisure time and there are more apt to be considerable periods of time when they cannot work at productive activities because of weather, lack of skills, lack of a market (especially true for the labor market), and other reasons. In short, it is harder for men to find some way to turn a few pesos in slack periods and spare time than it is for women. The economic sphere in which women operate, processing and selling in very small quantities through the market selling places, in the street, or at home, is closed to Zapotec men by custom. When the women in the houshold cannot process and sell for whatever reason, income from agricultural production will decrease to the extent that it must be sold wholesale in its raw state.

Processing–Vending Related to Other Household Duties

The processing–vending role of women must compete with a multitude of other household tasks, of which the care of infants and toddlers takes precedence. Normally having learned her economic skills in her natal household, these are more or less held in reserve after marriage until the woman herself has a child or two old enough to share some of the burden of caring for children and household. Gradually, the young woman reactivates processing–vending skills she learned as a girl or develops new ones as opportunities present themselves. Young women with small children can earn a few pesos now and then if they must, but it is not until middle age that most women have a great deal of time to devote to income-producing activities. After about age sixty, failing health often curbs economic pursuits, but older women support themselves wholly or in part through vending as long as they are able. A rare elderly woman even supports herself by making and selling totopos regularly.

Tasks other than child care also demand attention from women of the household, cutting into the time which can be used to increase household income. But household tasks require rather less time in the Isthmus than might be expected, because of the tropical climate, cultural adaptations, and a few simple but significant technological advances such as the mechanical nixtamal mill, which saves a household six or eight woman-hours daily formerly devoted to grinding maize by hand. The advent of manufactured textiles and sewing machines also save many woman-hours previously spent in weaving and sewing by hand.[16] Probably the most burdensome household task is washing clothes by hand, but the amount of washing necessary for a family is greatly reduced by sleeping arrangements that require no sheets or other bedding (people sleep in hammocks or on woven mats), by the practice of drying the body with the hands after bathing and air-drying the hair which makes towels unnecessary, and by allowing babies and toddlers to go without clothing or diapers. Generally boys wear no clothing until they are five or six years of age except on special occasions and girls wear only a brief panty or skirt around the solar.

Food preparation time is vastly reduced by mechanical maize-grinding and the availability of ready-made tortillas and the whole range of other prepared foods the housewife can so easily and cheaply purchase from her neighbors. Most housewives prepare one "pot" per day, very often a pasta or rice-based stew with vegetables plus a few ounces of beef, fish, or shrimp added for flavor. Such a pot will feed the

---

[16]Handweaving, formerly common among the Isthmus Zapotecs, has almost disappeared in the past generation. A few old women still weave in San Jacinto where handwoven skirt lengths can still be purchased. A few elderly Juanecas continued to wear the old-fashioned handwoven wraparound skirt, but by 1985 none were to be seen.

family for the main midday meal and the lighter evening supper, augmented by tortillas, salsa, coffee, sweet rolls, cheese, and other items purchased in the market to the degree that the household has cash available for these extras. In poor households the stew may contain no meat or other protein and only a few vegetables, and will be augmented only by tortillas.

The market places serve Isthmus Zapotec households in two important ways then: as a source of additional income and as a very inexpensive and convenient source of ready-to-serve food items, a device which saves labor just as packaged pre-cooked foods do in our own culture.

Dishwashing is never a great problem in Isthmus Zapotec households, although the amount of dishes and utensils used tends to increase with income and social status. In the campesino household, families with small children may not use individual dishes at all but simply dine in a circle around the cooking pot from which the parents feed themselves and the little ones, using tortillas as the utensil. At most, there will be a small bowl, cup, and perhaps a spoon for each individual. Teaspoons are needed only for stirring sugar into hot coffee as a rule. Tortillas serve as eating utensils as well as napkins to wipe one's mouth and fingertips at the end of the meal. Unless the food is greasy, soiled dishes are merely rinsed in cold water and allowed to dry in the air. Grease is removed by adding a little soap powder to the unheated water. The cooking pot will probably be left to soak until it is needed the following day.

Since the house itself usually consists of a single windowless room used mainly for storing clothing and housing the household shrine and since the average solar contains very little furniture, cleaning is not an especially time-consuming task. Most of the household's activities take place in the open, shaded patio called the *enramada,* or on the roofed open *corredor* (veranda), the same size and directly in front of the enclosed room. The corredor and enramada usually require sweeping daily since garbage and refuse are dropped randomly during the day's activities. The enramada floor is invariably packed earth and sometimes the corredor floor is also. Packed earth floors will be sprinkled by hand once or twice a day by the tidy housekeeper to confine the dust to a tolerable level. All in all, keeping the solar clean requires at most an hour per day. Again the amount of time household tasks require tends to increase with income and social status as houses become larger and furnishings become more elaborate. The traditional Isthmus Zapotec campesino solar, while neither comfortable nor aesthetically pleasing by North American standards, demands little time or attention from its occupants.

Animals kept within the solar or fed from the solar belong to the women of the household who also care for them. These include pigs, chickens, turkeys, and occasionally, ducks but do not include oxen, although the latter are often kept within the house compound at night. Pigs may be penned in a corner of the solar but more commonly they are permitted to scavenge the streets, alleys, and river banks, returning to the solar to be fed scraps and a little maize in the evening. Usually the maize must be shelled by hand first, requiring as much as an hour if there are several large pigs. Chickens are also fed scraps and maize, but their care requires little time or effort since their numbers are few and they have the run of the solar. Chickens, the occasional eggs they produce, and pigs are rarely kept for household use. They are raised to be sold and, for the women, constitute a source of cash for emergencies which they feel is worth the effort and inconvenience. The men of the household sometimes complain about the pigs and chickens running about, saying it costs more to feed them than they are worth.

Ironing is a considerable task in some households and in others no ironing is done at all. This again depends on the income and social status of the household. The poorer campesino households have less clothing, and what is owned is usually worn unironed except for special occasions.

Women are also responsible for nursing care of sick and disabled members of the household, a burdensome task over long periods of time and one that occurs with shocking frequency because of the general low level of health and lack of modern medical treatment for the majority of the population.

CONCLUSION

In concluding the discussion of the division of labor by sex, the following points deserve emphasis:

1. Division of labor by sex is relatively strict.
2. Economic roles are generally complementary by sex.
3. Each sex has access to distinct spheres of economic actions not open to the other.
4. Men's economic roles are always considered more important than those of women, even in cases where the women's roles contribute the greater share to household income.
5. Because women have many other household duties which compete with and take precedence over income-producing activities, the latter are often short-term and intermittent compared to those of men.
6. One result of women's processing–vending role is that men's production is sold by women in very small quantities over a period of time, with the income spent immediately for food and other daily household requirements. To the extent that household production passes through women's hands, women are in a position to control the finances of the household but in practice day-to-day requirements of the household allow women little opportunity to employ such control advantageously, much less abuse it.

Juanecas sometimes use a phrase which I think typifies the Isthmus Zapotec woman's perception of her economic role. When she leaves the solar with something to sell in the market place she states, "Bueno, ya tengo que buscar la comida!" meaning she must sell what she takes to market in order to buy food for the next meal.

Women's Attitudes Toward Processing–Vending

Despite the importance of the processing–vending roles and the fact that some women obviously enjoy selling, Juanecas are ambivalent about the role. They invariably state that they find the role distasteful but an economic necessity. This ambivalence was demonstrated clearly when a small sample (forty-seven) of processor–vendors was asked how they would dispose of a hypothetical windfall of a few thousand pesos. Only two women suggested expanding their processing–

vending activities with the money. The others stated unequivocally that they would discontinue selling and simply stay at home, even though the proposed windfall was only sufficient to permit them to do so for a limited period of time, perhaps a year or two. Most women proposed spending money on improvements to the solar.

This unexpected negative attitude toward the processing–vending role stems, I believe, from peasant women's acceptance of middle-class elite mestizo values as the ideal. Local elite women seldom leave their solares, much less set foot in the market places. Servants do their shopping and errand running. On the rare occasions when they come to the central district, they are accompanied by servants to carry their purchases. Middle-class mestizo women may do their own shopping, but they never sell in the market places or on the streets.[17] They do not carry heavy burdens and never carry burdens on their heads, both more or less necessities for processor–vendors. Peasant women are acutely aware that their market activities mark them as "low class" to the mestizo population. They rationalize their economic role as a necessity of their unfavorable economic circumstances even when this may not be true in particular cases.[18]

A second factor is the low esteem of marketing activities compared with other economic roles. With few exceptions, marketing is thought of as an unskilled job anyone can do. Informants often state that they sell in the market "because my mother didn't teach me any skills" or "because I was an orphan and had no one to teach me anything." A relatively simple specialization such as seamstress commands great respect and is thought by most women to be much more difficult to master than is the case. This is probably because sewing machines, while not rare, are not available to every woman.[19] A third reason for the low prestige of processing–vending may relate to its small scale and consequent low level of profit for most vendors, but this would not explain why owning a tiendita is a status symbol although often less profitable than selling in the market places. Again, this seems to relate to the prevalence of mestizo values as ideals.

Campesinos' Perception of Their Economic Position

Although Isthmus Zapotec campesinos are relatively more prosperous than many other indigenous peasant populations in Latin America, they tend to think of themselves as economically and socially disadvantaged. A characteristic attitude of peasants in many parts of the world, this belief is often an accurate assessment of their situation. Yet Isthmus Zapotec peasants are well aware that they are not on the bottom of the economic ladder even locally. There are certain types of work no Zapotec peasant will accept—for example, street peddling by men, laundering and

[17]Middle-class and even some upper-class women earn extra income by sewing, knitting, or selling Avon products, but they do so from their homes. One mestizo woman, an ex-schoolteacher, had begun selling Avon house to house part of the time, always accompanied by her husband.

[18]There are a few San Juan families who are very well-to-do by regional standards, but the women continue the processing–vending role and continue carrying burdens on their heads even though such "low-class" behavior is not an economic necessity.

[19]Several San Juan women conduct sewing schools in their homes where girls are taught, for a fee, basic sewing techniques and the use of a treadle sewing machine. Seamstresses often train apprentices, which also involves an initial fee on the part of the apprentice. Seamstresses may employ from one to four apprentices, some of them young muxe men.

housework for hire by women. Destitute families will sometimes allow a daughter to accept a live-in position with a wealthy family, preferably in Mexico City. Such girls do not expect and will not tolerate treatment as servants. Unless they are treated as daughters of the family (and they are often related to the employing family), they will not remain no matter what the economic pressure. Well-to-do families in the Isthmus have a great deal of trouble acquiring and keeping satisfactory servant girls. The most prosperous San Juan households employ a servant or two when they can secure them, but prefer *vallistas* (natives of the Valley of Oaxaca), who are harder working and less demanding. Laundresses, when they can be found, are almost always vallistas from the squatter settlements.

Zapotec peasants recognize as clearly beneath them two major groups: (1) the vallistas, which in local usage includes all the itinerant, rootless population which drifts in and out of the Isthmus, whatever their origin; and (2) the Mareños, the coastal peoples whom Zapotecs have dominated through trade relations for centuries.

Recognized as above themselves are the petty officials, clerks, schoolteachers, anyone who does not have to soil himself in his work or work with his hands.[20] Economically such persons are often far poorer than the well-to-do peasant families, but social status hinges on much more than mere economic resources. Clearly, the regional urban middle class and elites, even those of Zapotec origin, are all considered above the campesinos on the social scale.

Acutally, then, Zapotec campesinos occupy a middle position in the regional social status hierarchy, a position reflected in atttudes toward social inferiors but not in their perception of their status with respect to those above them.

[20]Even the use of the word *trabajo* is taboo in upper-class circles. Since I was a North American I was automatically placed as upper class. At first when people asked me, "What have you been doing today?" I replied, "working." One day an old man, head of one of the most prominent families in El Centro, took me aside. "Don't say you are working. That is such a vulgar word. Just say you are *paseando*" (idly passing time) was his fatherly advice.

5 / Rhythms of Zapotec Peasant Life

For most individuals in every culture the day-to-day routine tends toward monotony and repetition. Isthmus Zapotec peasants are not exceptions. If anything, the eternal sameness of temperature, the ceaseless agricultural work cycle and marketing activities, and the paucity of recreational diversions add to the monotony of daily living. Boredom is especially trying for young people who have so few opportunities to use creatively youth's boundless energy and curiosity. But if there is a numbing tedium to daily life, there is also a sense of foreboding and insecurity which hovers over people's lives like a storm cloud on the horizon, promising to break the monotony—but in disastrous ways. This chapter introduces the reader to the basic rhythms of life—the life cycle and the daily routine, broken now and then by the annual ritual cycle and the rites of passage. The aspirations, anxieties, ideals, and values which shape people's behavior, adding flesh to the skeletons of life's routines, are described in later chapters.

DAILY ROUTINE

For most households in San Juan Evangelista the day begins early, often well before daylight.[1] Coffee and sweet rolls or totopos break the night's fast, with the main morning meal eaten later, around 7 A.M., after morning chores are completed and before the day's remaining tasks are begun. This meal is almost invariably purchased in the local plazita because leftovers from the previous day cannot be consumed with safety. If the man of the house is going to the fields, he may have left at daylight, carrying food for the morning and noon meals, or if the distance is not excessive a child may be sent to the field later with a hot meal.

Women do the daily shopping immediately before or immediately after breakfast so that the food for the noon meal will have several hours to cook. If tortillas or totopos are to be made, a daughter of the house will take the grain, already soaked overnight, to the mill to be ground before breakfast. Women going to the El Centro market to sell will leave the house between 6 A.M. and 7 A.M. Those going to San Jacinto may not leave until 8 A.M. or 9 A.M. or even later, since that market is active

---

[1]In the household where I lived for several months the regular hour was 4 A.M., about two hours before daylight. A number of households—for example, butchers of beef and pork—begin the day regularly between 1 A.M. and 2 A.M., while many others may do so from time to time in connection with specific activities such as going to el monte for firewood and lumber.

all day. The woman who remains in the solar will tidy up, sweeping out the fruit rinds, pits, and other discards from the previous day's activities and sprinkling the packed earth with water. She prepares the pot for the day and perhaps washes a few pieces of clothing. In some households, handling fruit and drying fish and shrimp are time-consuming daily chores.[2] Whatever time remains before the midday meal will be devoted to skills the woman possesses which provide income for the household—making tortillas or totopos, sewing *huipiles* (women's traditional blouse) by machine, embroidering, or perhaps making paper flowers. Girls between 10 and 15 who do not attend school will usually be put to selling something from the doorway or street corner near their homes—homemade beverages, sliced oranges, cucumber or pineapple slices, mangoes, *queeze'* or other snack foods. Boys of comparable age are more apt to be enrolled in school and to attend more or less regularly, but if not they will be helping their father with his tasks.

The midday meal is taken between 1 P.M. and 2 P.M. and is rarely a family affair. One or two persons may eat at the same time, but it is more by coincidence than by plan. The man of the house and the sons will be served when they arrive home. Women and girls who remain at home eat when they are hungry and others eat when they return from the market place. Commonly, a lone diner will not eat at a dining table, if indeed there is one in the household, but will seat himself on a *butaca* (low stool), using a regular straight-back chair for his table.

The afternoon siesta extends from the midday meal to about 4 P.M. for most people, but often people do not actually nap, or do so for only a short period. The remaining siesta time may be spent in visiting or doing some light sedentary work such as embroidery. If men are working far from home they take the siesta in the field, not returning to the pueblo until dusk or after. If they are working near home they will probably try to complete their day's work before 1 P.M. and return to the solar for the noon meal and siesta time, taking up some activity around the solar afterward.

After 4 P.M. when businesses reopen, household activities also pick up. Women who sell for the supper trade make preparations for going to the market place from which they will return at about 8 P.M. Other women feed the household animals, carry firewood in for the morning, put grain to soak, and prepare the evening meal, which often entails only buying tortillas to go with the leftover midday stew. Water jars are filled if the solar has piped water. If not, boys will be sent to the nearest source from which water can be carried. Isthmus Zapotecs are personally fastidious people, normally bathing at least once daily. Women and girls often do this during siesta hours so that their thick hair, shampooed almost daily, dries before nightfall. Women bathe in the solar, dipping water from a large olla with half a gourd and pouring it over the body. Men will probably bathe in the river or irrigation canal on their way home from the fields, watering their oxen and washing both the ox team and cart at the same time. The man's last chore of the day is feeding his oxen, usually with fodder cut in the field and carried home on the oxcart.

Even if the solar has electricity, the family will probably retire at dusk or very

---

[2]For example, bananas are placed in a darkened room or storage space to ripen and must be turned daily. About every other day the ripe bananas must be selected from each stalk and removed to be sold or eaten. Drying fish and shrimp entails putting the products in the full sun, adding salt daily, and covering the drying tables at night with light cloths to keep off moisture and pests.

San Juan Woman Resting (1982)

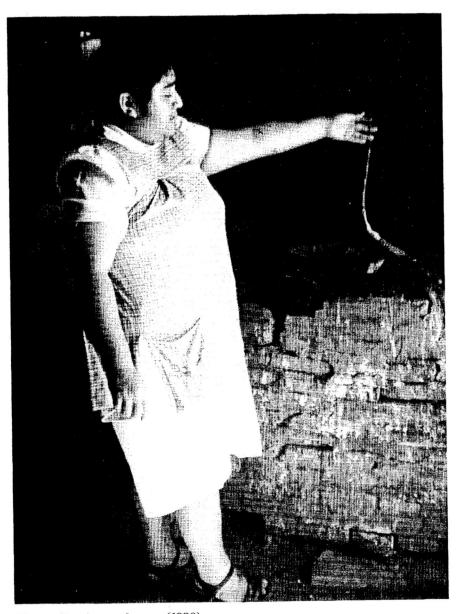

Woman Singeing an Iguana (1990)

shortly thereafter.[3] Artificial light is more useful in the cool house before dawn when the day begins than in the evenings when everyone is tired and the day's heat lingers.

[3]According to the official 1960 census only slightly more than 5 percent of 1,130 households in the municipio had electricity, flush toilet, shower, and drain. In 1967 I estimated about half the households had electricity but the proportion of households with all the four above-mentioned conveniences had improved only slightly. By 1990 most households had electricity, shower, and drainage and a considerable number had flush toilets.

This routine is broken slightly on Saturday nights when young people stream to El Centro to attend one of the two cinemas or, on Sunday evenings, to join the *paseo*. Otherwise, Sundays are less exceptional than in many places because the market places remain open, as do a number of El Centro businesses. Sunday mornings (as well as Thursdays) find women and girls walking to the cemeteries with basins and buckets of fresh flowers on their heads to be left at the graves of loved ones. Sunday afternoons are traditionally the time when married daughters visit their mother's solar. Women who sell regularly in the market places do so seven days a week, taking an occasional day off as needed but usually not once a week and almost certainly not Sunday, the day market sales are best.

The important breaks in routine are those marked by fiestas—honoring the saints or marking individual rites of passage. Women especially look forward eagerly to the fiestas, perhaps because they have almost no other socially acceptable form of recreation. Fiestas are the only occasions when it is permissible for women to dance, drink beer, gossip, show off their best clothing, and enjoy themselves in the company of other women outside a workaday context. Not only the fiesta itself, but preparation for it, which is often initiated a month earlier, mean breaks in routine and social interaction for women. Even those women who are prevented from attending the fiesta itself because of mourning or other reasons can participate in the cooperative food preparation activities. Men sometimes complain that the womenfolk are too much involved in fiestas, and indeed they do contribute more cooperative labor and often more money than their menfolk.

Men find recreation in drinking and conversation in the cantinas and around the peripheries of the fiestas, but men who attend fiestas seem to treat it less as recreation than ritual, a religious and social duty, a time for ritual drinking and cigarette smoking which inevitably ends in alcoholic stupor and probably, for most men, massive hangovers.

Market activities have often been mentioned as having recreational aspects for peasant women. There is no doubt that seasonal selling trips to Oaxaca or even simply to El Centro or San Jacinto provide welcome relief from routine for some women, and teen-age girls certainly anticipate trips to the market places or any other errands offering an escape from the solar, but I think the recreational, pleasurable aspects of market selling have been much overplayed with respect to Isthmus Zapotec women. Selling often involves a great deal of hard work, personal discomfort, and boredom which women would avoid if they could.

Young people seem to have less recreational activities than adults since the fiestas are ritual affairs of adult members of the community with youth having few formalized fiesta roles. Groups of teen-age girls or boys sometimes plan Sunday picnics in the orchards and more rarely at the beach. Occasionally mixed groups with chaperones hire a pickup truck and driver for a Sunday outing. Then there are the movie houses and Sunday night paseo attended mostly by the young people. The river, the pueblo's traditional playground, has lost its attraction in recent years because damming for irrigation and flood control has reduced it to a series of malodorous stagnant pools during much of the year.

THE LIFE CYCLE

There is little doubt that parenthood is one of the central values of Isthmus Zapotec culture. Without children, neither women nor men can achieve true adult status, and traditionally the more children parents successfully reared, the greater the chances of a secure old age.[4] A 30-year-old informant explained his lack of enthusiasm for fiestas with,

> "I have nothing against the fiestas. But how can I go and sit there all day among the men when everybody knows I have no children! It makes me feel like a child myself!"

Although unmarried, this man was head of the household of his widowed mother. One marries primarily to produce children and sterility is considered one of the greatest tragedies that can befall a woman. In the late 1970s and 1980s, though, Zapotec families have become smaller. Now it is considered sufficient to rear two, at most three, children. Families of five to seven minor children (the old pattern) are now rare.

Birth to Marriage

Pregnancies usually occur within a few months after marriage. Few taboos are observed. Unless one is ill, work is carried on as usual. Cheese and totopos are thought to be especially good for expectant mothers but there is little evidence that the nomal diet is restricted or changed to a significant degree. There are no formal restrictions on sexual intercourse during pregnancy and in some cases at least it continues almost to the termination of the gestation period.[5]

Babies are born at home with a local *partera* (midwife), close women relatives, and the father in attendance. The father's presence is of great importance and is in striking contrast to the general puritanical attitudes toward sex and modesty that prevail. The husband comforts and encourages his wife during labor, and after delivery it is the father's duty to place the afterbirth in a new pottery jar which he then covers securely and buries under the floor of the house. If this is not properly

---

[4]Raising children to adulthood is what counts. Often people forget to mention children under three years to census takers and other outsiders because they are not considered full members of the household until some time after age three. This oversight accounts for the population pyramid with a smaller base than would be expected, rather than a decrease in the birth rate.

[5]An informant expressed the opinion that Mongolian spots, a blue area which sometimes occurs at the base of the spine in newborn American Indian and Asiatic babies, were caused by the father's penis bruising the child before birth.

done, the baby's eyes will become infected.[6] The parturient woman usually reclines on a canvas cot, but sometimes she assumes a half-reclining position on two benches placed a few inches apart. Local parteras without formal training charge $30 while those with some formal training may charge as much as $200. Medical doctors are not called unless complications arise and may charge up to $600. Very few women consult a medical doctor during pregnancy. Shortly after birth the father may invite a few neighbors and friends for a little fiesta, especially if it is a first child or a first son. Mother and child rest on a cot while neighbors and relatives prepare and enjoy the fiesta.

In 1975 I found that, while there was one medical doctor, three government-trained midwives, and a half-dozen traditional Zapotec midwives practicing in the pueblo, most women went to two of the traditional midwives, one an 80-year-old blind woman who employed a young woman as her apprentice-assistant, and the other the 56-year-old daughter of the 80-year-old. The daughter was the overwhelming favorite midwife, had been practicing for about 30 years, had attended a workshop on midwivery with a translator, and claimed that she had never lost a newborn. She complained that she could do much better at caring for mother and child if the mothers would come in to see her periodically before the birth. Almost none of them did so. By 1990 a number of families had access to the Social Security hospital through a husband's work in the oil refinery but many still preferred the traditional at-home births with midwife.

Ideally mother and child do not leave the solar for 40 days, but the mother usually resumes her normal household duties after about two weeks. Some families think it is important to have the baby baptized within the first month or two of life. A god-parent of the same sex as the child takes the infant to the church for baptism without the presence of the parents. Some families put off baptism indefinitely as long as the child appears in good health, but he will eventually be baptized during the first four or five years of life. First communion is also variable. Some first communions take place as early as one month of age while others are postponed until the child is ten years old, often depending on the availability of a willing sponsor. Again parents do not attend. Fiestas for baptisms and communions are rare, and when they occur, they are very small family affairs with only the godparent and perhaps a few other friends and relatives.

Babies are nursed for from one to two years and are not fed supplementally until they are at least a year old. The mother nurses the baby whenever it cries. As the baby's food demands increase beyond the mother's capacity to produce milk, the baby may become fussy and have to be nursed every few minutes, but the trouble is rarely diagnosed as hunger. Bottle feeding is still rare.

Although figures are absent, infant mortality is high in San Juan Evangelista;

[6]A family who prided themselves on their modernity and lack of superstition had the extraordinary experience of the seventh child being born within hours after the grandmother died in the solar. As soon as labor commenced, the mother moved to a nearby empty solar accompanied by her youngest adult sister who had purposely stayed away from the solar until then so as to remain free from the contamination of *calor*. About three days after the birth they moved back into the solar. Meantime, the father had been prevented from burying the afterbirth because of his contamination. Once back in the home solar, the baby was placed under the continuous surveillance of the saint, *Corazon Sagrado de Jesus*. Nonetheless, the baby's eyes became badly infected, the first of the seven children to suffer such a fate.

however, it has certainly dropped since the advent of antibiotics. The crucial periods are the first three months of life and the months after weaning, especially if weaning occurs as early as one year. Until age two or three, the possibility of death is a real one even today. The child's health is the direct responsibility of its mother, and when a death occurs, gossip circulates that the mother did not feed the child properly or that she neglected to protect it from the *calor* of the dead, from *ojo* (the eye) or *aire* (bad air) or other supernaturally caused illness. A prudent mother cares for the baby herself unless she has daughters old enough to share the responsibility. Children are rarely allowed outside the solar without an adult until they are five or six years old.[7]

Isthmus Zapotec babies are never carried in rebozos as in other parts of Mexico but only in the arms or on the hip. The explanation probably lies in the practice of keeping babies confined to the solar. Except for frequency of nursing, infant care is relatively simple. No diapers are used but a piece of a discarded skirt is kept under the small baby to soak up moisture and protect her skin from the prickly *ixtle* (hemp) hammocks and woven mats. These cloths can be quickly rinsed, dried, and reused so that only two or three, not dozens, are required. Mothers try to keep the genitalia of baby girls covered when men and boys are present. Otherwise no clothing is required. When a little girl is able to walk she will be dressed in homemade cotton panties. Boys normally wear no clothing until age six or so unless weather makes a light shirt mandatory.

Weaning between the ages of one and two is probably one of the leading factors in early childhood morbidity because a common result of early weaning is extreme malnutrition. I suspect that the short nursing period is a relatively recent development. The child of a year, unable to masticate her food, is weaned mainly on tortillas, pozole, atole, and coffee with sugar. The diet is certain to be deficient in protein and calcium. Although native local products that would provide an adequate diet are available and cheap (except milk), mothers are ignorant of nutrition and the effects of inadequate diet on children. They tend to blame childhood troubles on supernatural phenomena. As a consequence, the two-year-old child who was a chubby, bright-eyed infant a year earlier will probably be thin, suffering from recurrent diarrhea and fever, and exhibiting signs of rickets. Very often children between two and three years old suffer from open infected sores which may begin as mosquito bites but because of malnutrition and low disease resistance are easily infected and slow to heal. The malady is thought of as a natural occurrence of childhood just as the ancient Greeks thought the symptoms of rickets were part of the normal development pattern. If a child's condition deteriorates or seems chronic, the mother, after having tried a series of folk remedies, will probably consult a medical doctor who invariably prescribes massive dosages of vitamins, some form of calcium (usually canned milk), an egg, and fresh tomato juice daily. Typically the vitamins will be administered until the baby shows signs of improvement if the family can afford them. The food products, so much cheaper and locally available, may be attempted once or twice, but if the baby rejects them they are discontinued because women see no connection between health and food or between food as a source of the same vitamins purchased in bottles. Although such severe

[7]See footnote 4.

cases of malnutrition are common, not all infants exhibit symptoms of malnutrition. The differences are probably to be explained by differences in weaning practices and family income and eating habits. One family with seven children, all in glowing health, began to buy canned milk for the two youngest after the older siblings learned in school of the importance of milk in the young child's diet.

Toilet training is accomplished between the ages of two and three with little apparent effort. When the mother decides the child is old enough to understand her instructions, she explains where he is to go to urinate and defecate (usually a remote corner of the solar) and within a few weeks or months training is complete. If the child is slow to learn no pressure is put on him unless he proves inordinately slow, when shame may be employed.

During the early years the mother and other female household members are mainly responsible for socializing the child because adult men are normally away from the solar during most of the child's waking hours. Although some informants claimed mothers were harsh disciplinarians, scores of observations of mothers and children of various ages in many different situations did not bear out the claim. The most severe action toward a small child I ever witnessed was a mild scolding. Two reports of severe beatings administered by mothers involved teen-age daughters. Informants were very critical of these actions by mothers, even though they acknowledged that the girls probably provoked the attacks by improper behavior. But these were extreme cases and obviously infrequent. Although some beating of wives and children by drunken husbands occurs, corporal punishment of children of any age by either parent is not condoned, nor is wife-beating.

Isthmus Zapotecs are often overly permissive and benign in child training by North American middle-class standards. Children sometimes appear boisterous and unruly, but since they are largely confined to the solar, their behavior does not annoy the neighbors. A belief that children can become ill and even die of *tristeza* (sadness) if they are harshly disciplined or not permitted to do as they wish is at least partly responsible for parental permissiveness.

Boys of all ages are allowed a great deal more freedom than are girls, and fewer demands and responsibilities are placed on them than on girls and usually at a later age. If there are several younger children, a daughter will begin to assume some responsibility for household duties by age six or seven. She will often not be allowed to attend school because the mother depends on her help, especially if the family is poor. Care of infants and toddlers by older siblings occurs only within the solar and only under the close supervision of the mother or other adult. Children are never seen in the streets with infant siblings strapped to their backs as in some parts of Mesoamerica. Boys have few duties around the house, and the probability that they will attend school at least to age 12 or so is much greater than for girls. After age 12 the boy can begin to work in the fields with his father. The large majority of campesino families still considers even a minimal formal education for daughters an unnecessary frill, but that is gradually changing.

Girls begin very early to learn to be shrewd shoppers, to make change, and to add and subtract small sums mentally. By the age of seven, girls are sent now and again to the plazita to purchase food. When they return home, they must give an accounting of how much they paid for each item, along with the leftover change, to the mother. If she thinks the onion is too small for the price, the tomatoes of poor quality, or if the girl is short a tortilla (fifteen for a peso), the mother will probably scold her mildly. Sometimes a child will be sent back to the vendor to return an item and get a refund. Vendors, all women of the pueblo, are usually very tolerant of such exchanges and return the money without question. Gradually the girl gains enough experience to be sent to sell tortillas in the market place or sliced oranges from the doorway of the solar. This type of selling may begin as early as age ten. The money she earns is not hers but belongs to the household and is turned over to the mother. Boys, though often sent on errands by their fathers, do little buying and no selling and, therefore, receive less experience in mental arithmetic than girls.

After age six, boys spend many hours playing in groups in the streets. Girls are seldom allowed to play outside the solar. Nor is it proper for older girls and women to be seen on the streets alone unless they are clearly on an errand. Girls are taught not to loiter on their way to and from the market place and are subject to reprimand if they do so. After puberty, girls are sent on fewer trips to the market places, especially during the early teens. Virginity at marriage is still expected, and although the girl's moral character reflects on the entire family, the daughter's behavior is mainly the mother's responsibility. In the early teens when girls are apt to be giddy and irresponsible they are kept under close surveillance "until she gets her reason" as women explain it. During these years girls spend most of their time learning the more intricate household arts such as cooking and making tortillas and totopos, sewing, and embroidery. By the time a girl is 17 she should be able to run her own household efficiently, although she will probably not have the opportunity to do so until some years after marriage. Relations between mother and daughter from puberty to marriage often become strained because of the tight restrictions placed on the girl while younger children and older brothers enjoy much more freedom and less responsibility.

Although there are exceptions such as the family with five sons and one daughter, boys appear to be accorded preferential treatment by both parents in a number of ways. In education, parents are more willing to sacrifice for boys because sons are expected to be responsible for supporting aged parents. Sisters of whatever age are supposed to be subordinate to brothers until marriage. There is often considerable rivalry between siblings of opposite sex, increasing as they grow to adulthood. Girls resent brothers because the boy has almost complete freedom just at the age when her movements are being severely restricted. Then, at the same time, the brother may take seriously his responsibility for the good conduct of his sisters, perhaps exaggerating the culturally sanctioned role as "protector" until the girls view him as oppressor rather than protector. Again, the girl may resent family finances being drained to educate a son while she works very hard with little reward helping the household meet such expenses.[8]

Courtship and Marriage

From puberty until about age 16, girls may get few opportunities to meet and talk with their age-mates of the opposite sex. Loitering or talking to boys in the

---

[8]One 18-year-old girl, within hearing of her mother, complained bitterly that all the mother's jewelry was going to pay for the medical education of her brother, jewelry that would normally be part of her dowry. "By the time I marry we will all be paupers!" she lamented.

streets is firmly discouraged, and every adult woman in the pueblo considers it her duty to report such misconduct to the girl's mother. When a girl is about 16, she will not be suddenly set free but she will be allowed to attend a public fiesta on occasion where she will be under the watchful eye of an aunt or grandmother if not directly chaperoned. Younger siblings, cousins, or nieces and nephews often accompany teen-age girls, even on errands. Finally, the girl, accompanied by several of these young relatives and maybe a girl friend or two, will be allowed to attend the Sunday evening paseos in El Centro now and then.[9] The paseo in El Centro is a rather informal affair in which persons of all ages, even whole families, stroll around the plaza, those at the outer edge in one direction and those on the inner side in the opposite direction. There is much dropping out and visiting by couples with small children and middle-aged couples. Adults seem mostly to be mestizo middle-class couples from El Centro. The paseo attracts young people because it is about the only way one can look over the field of prospective novios and perhaps even manage to exchange a few words. This is the usual way courtships are initiated, although nowadays the coeducational secondary schools offer another avenue. Traditionally, families arranged marriages, but modern young people have more freedom to choose their own mates. Nonetheless, most courtships are slow, cautious affairs because the girl's parents may stop it at any point simply by confining the girl to the solar for an indefinite period, even months.

After a few exchanges at paseo, at school, or in the streets, the boy will muster his courage sufficiently to wait in the street near the girl's home Sunday evenings until he finally hits an evening when she is being allowed out. This is a critical point in the proceedings for the boy. No words need be exchanged, but if the girl allows him to accompany her, they are novios. The suitor hopes to keep the girl's parents from discovering his intentions until he is at least sure of the girl's feelings. If all goes well, he gradually becomes more self-assured and courageous enough to spend most of his free evenings waiting outside the girl's door out of sight in the hope that she will emerge on some errand. By this time the affair may have been in progress for months, perhaps more than a year. The girl's parents have long since become aware of the novio's presence and given their tacit approval, all the while pretending total ignorance. Traditionally, the courtship concludes with representatives of the suitor presenting a petition to the girl's parents on his behalf. In the old days, the consent of the girl's parents initiated a series of ceremonial exchanges between the two families. Today the novio's father, godfather, or other adult male kin may talk with the girl's parents, but the ceremonial exchanges have been almost abandoned. Once the courtship is initiated, breaking off the affair by the couple themselves is considered unfortunate, especially for the girl because such action is thought to reflect on her character.[10]

Marriage banns are posted and announced on the public address system a month before the wedding mass. Since church weddings are not recognized by the Mexican government, the novios will probably be married *por civil* in El Centro Saturday afternoon before the church wedding. Brides wear their embroidered *traje*

[9]The paseo derives from sixteenth-century Spain.

[10]A middle-aged informant who considered that a novio had jilted her after initiating a courtship when she was 15 years old still refused to speak to the man, although both lived in San Juan and frequently passed in the streets.

on this occasion rather than the bridal gown and may or may not be accompanied by their *padrinos* (godparents). If the parents are well-to-do, they may pay the civil officials to come to their solar Saturday afternoon where a small fiesta takes place after the civil ceremony.

All marriages in the church are performed at 8 A.M. mass on Sundays. In San Juan Evangelista as many as six couples may be married at the same mass, although one or two is more usual. The novios are accompanied by their padrinos. As with baptisms, parents of the couple usually do not attend the wedding mass. At the end of the mass, each newlywed couple emerges from the church and pauses briefly for photographs previously arranged. A band is waiting just outside the gate, hired by the novio's father. As soon as the couple emerges from the church compound, their musicians strike up the local version of a wedding march and lead the newlyweds and padrinos, followed by the wedding party, through the streets of the pueblo to the home of the novio's parents. Even if cars and taxis are available, it is not proper for the newlyweds or the wedding guests to ride. Everyone walks even if the distance is more than a mile. Their arrival at the virilocal solar, announced by a fiery barrage of *cohetes* (fireworks), initiates a day-long fiesta that is actually a series of ritual acts performed by specific groups of persons at specific times, interlaced with intervals of dancing and drinking (beer for women, *mezcal* toasting and cigarette smoking for men). The novios' roles in the fiesta are mostly as passive observers, seated all the long, hot day in their wedding attire at the novios' table flanked by their padrinos, rising only briefly at various times to perform their part of a ritual act such as kissing and passing to each guest a paper flower or kneeling to receive the benediction of the guests. Until midday the wedding guests are elder kinsmen and compadres of the novio's parents and *los invitados* (invited guests) of the padrinos. The bride's kin group arrives about noon and departs about two hours later, having fulfilled their part of the ceremony. At about 4 P.M. the padrinos and their invited guests depart, leaving the newlyweds with the novio's kin.

Traditionally, the marriage had to be consummated in the presence of witnesses, usually elderly female kin of the novio. That custom seems to have been completely discontinued in favor of allowing the couple more privacy, but the groom's kin group still expects to wait in the enramada until the consummation at which time the groom emerges to present his mother with a handkerchief stained with evidence of the bride's virginity. Then there is a great deal of excitement and rejoicing and the groom's mother heads the procession taking a basket filled with red flowers and containing the blood-stained cloth to the bride's solar. The hour may be late but the band leads the way as cohetes mark the procession's departure. Mercifully, the newlyweds are spared this final procession. The bride's kin group, especially the women led by her mother, will celebrate with a fiesta of their own the following day, at which time girls pass through the market places with baskets of red flowers, sprinkling red confetti on the heads of vendors and customers alike as an announcement of a successful conclusion to the marriage rites.

The more or less public consummation of the marriage and the great publicity which accompanies it in the traditional ceremony are considered by young people to be a horrendous ordeal. For the girls especially it is a traumatic experience they never forget, but boys too prefer to avoid the public embarrassment. Fortunately there is an alternative in the form of marriage *por robar*, or elopement. No statistics are available, but my impression is that the number of elopements at least equals the number of traditional marriages. Whether this is a stable condition of some duration or whether elopements are becoming more prevalent than formerly is unknown.

Elopement involves the couple agreeing secretly to meet at a designated time and place. They go to the novio's home where he hides the girl from his parents as long as possible, usually a few hours. When the parents discover the elopement, they go immediately to talk with the girl's parents—even if the hour is 3 A.M.—to persuade her parents to accept an arrangement. If they are agreeable, the girl may return home the next day and begin making preparations for a church wedding a month hence. If the parents are opposed, the couple will probably remain together, hoping for a later reconciliation with her parents.[11]

When the bride goes to the solar of her husband immediately after the marriage, she goes to her new home, where the couple will remain perhaps until two or three children are born, perhaps until the old people die and the husband inherits the solar. The first years of marriage can be an uncomfortable time for a young wife in a strange household under the thumb of a mother-in-law who may have been a complete stranger to her. Some brides cannot adjust and persuade their husband to establish a neolocal residence as soon as possible. Although divorce is not recognized by the church, it is legally acceptable. Some brides take this route to freedom after failing to persuade the husband to make a new home. The bride and her children, if any, return to her natal home where it is her brother's responsibility to help her. Divorce is still uncommon in San Juan Evangelista but frequent in El Centro. Women are also learning that they can petition the courts for child support from the father even if there was no marriage ceremony, and they are usually not shy about doing so.

A surprising number of wives do adjust remarkably well to living with their mothers-in-law, and sometimes very strong bonds of affection form between them over the years. Frequently, the mother-in-law sides with the wife against her own son, especially when his behavior is obviously at the root of the trouble. Padrinos of the newlyweds are supposed to act as advisers and mediators between the couple all of their married life. In event of serious problems, the padrinos as well as elder relatives will probably be called in to arbitrate before legal action is taken by either side.

A wife's status increases as her family grows, reaching its highest when she herself becomes a mother-in-law to her sons' wives. A woman without daughters-in-law is unfortunate because she will be either left alone in old age or have to depend on her daughters. If all the daughters are married there is a conflict of duties. Care for the husband's aged parents takes precedence ideally but not always in practice. Elderly parents worry a great deal about nursing care in old age which is often required and must be provided by members of the household.

In Zapotec culture elders of both sexes are highly respected and treated with

[11]An elder daughter of a large family eloped with only six weeks of school remaining before she was to graduate with a secondary diploma. The family had made great sacrifices for her education and was bitterly disappointed. The eloping couple did not contact the parents for three months, hiding out in the novio's solar in another town. Reconciliation had to await the birth of the first child more than a year later.

great courtesy. No parent is willfully neglected, and parents normally retain a great deal of authority over their families as long as they live, especially over those who live in the parents' solar.

The best period of life for the individual begins in middle age, for this is the time when children begin to help substantially in supporting the household, when parents may have more time and money to devote to the fiesta system and making various *promesas* (religious vows) and commitments which will add to status and prestige. For women, at least, freedom from some of the severe cultural restrictions begins in middle age after the childbearing years end. As the woman grows older, she can go anywhere alone, attending fiestas as often as she wants and can afford, and she has daughters-in-law and grandchildren to augment her status. Men's and women's roles are not as sharply drawn as previously, and the sexes are allowed free interchange and interaction for the first time in their lives. Elderly men and women, perhaps lifelong compadres or neighbors, lend one another comfort and moral support during the trying periods of illness and death. These tender relationships between the aged are among the most poignant in Isthmus Zapotec culture.[12]

Death, and Rituals for the Dead

Isthmus Zapotecs do not have North Americans' exaggerated aversion to death. Indeed, Isthmus Zapotecs seem more preoccupied with death than is generally true in Mesoamerica, although the subject is very much a part of everyday thought and habits everywhere. In el Istmo, death is no stranger even to small children, who hear their elders discuss and refer to it every day in numberless contexts. Not unexpectedly, a great deal of ritual centers around death and honoring deceased kin. Dead kin, especially parents, continue to exert great influence on the living, frequently receiving as much attention for a while as during life. Women are especially attentive to deceased parents and husbands, carrying flowers to their graves once or twice a week sometimes for years. Households often undertake heavy financial burdens to fulfill obligations to deceased members through the series of rites called *mixa gue'tu'*.

Although natural causes of illness and death are recognized, strong emotions such as fright and anger, witchcraft, evil eye, los aires, spirits, calor of the dead, and the imbalance of hot and cold influences on the body's humors also are believed to cause illness which can lead to death.[13] For curing, most people try home remedies first. If there is no improvement in the condition, women may call a *curandera* (native curer) for themselves and their children; the curandera diagnoses the cause of the illness and treats it accordingly. Nowadays medical doctors and druggists are usually the first choices to consult if one has enough cash. Illnesses

---

[12]An elderly woman, bedridden for a year, was visited by an old man, a neighbor of years long past, whom she had not seen for several years. The sickroom was full of family and several other visitors. The old man spent the better part of an hour leaning over his former neighbor, whispering in her ear, after which he greeted the other persons briefly and departed. I witnessed a number of similar instances of tenderness, concern, and confidence between nonrelated elderly persons of opposite sex, especially when one of them was in poor health.

[13]Most of these beliefs derive from sixteenth-century Europe, but some elements may have been similar in both the Old World and the New World folk beliefs.

that do not readily respond to medicines and treatments will most likely be attributed to supernatural causes, and efforts will continue to identify the responsible supernatural agent. Men are thought to be more immune to many of the supernaturally and emotionally caused ailments than women and children and therefore do not consult native curers often.[14] As an informant put it, "We (women and children) need the curanderas a lot because we are desirable. We get sick so much because people are always admiring us." Men are not thought to be attractive and desirable in the same way as women and children, but they too sometimes suffer illness caused by anger, fright, witchcraft, and spirits of the dead. Men are prone to consult the druggist for medicine after home remedies fail, then medical doctors, but the women of the household will eventually prevail on them to consult a curer too, especially if improvement is not apparent. Recently, people have begun to look upon antibiotics as miracle drugs, using them indiscriminately for the smallest problem.[15]

No Zapotec lives alone or dies alone by choice, and few do so by chance. While ill persons and babies are protected from direct or indirect contact with corpses because they can be adversely affected by the calor of the latter, sick people are never isolated from other persons because they are sick. Indeed, there seems to be a conscious effort to include the gravely ill member in all the household affairs by placing her in a central spot where she can observe and hear everything. Inevitably, a visitor to the household, even a complete stranger such as an anthropologist, will be presented a seat where the invalid can see and hear the visitor. In view of the general suspicion that surrounds strangers, I found this custom unexpected. Perhaps the stranger is not viewed as a danger to a dying person because desire, admiration, and envy are thought to be absent.

When death seems imminent, relatives and neighbors, including children (except babies), crowd around the dying person, the women weeping, leaning over the victim to detect and observe signs of respiration. This knot of people around a dying person is sometimes so dense that breathing is difficult for a healthy person caught in the press of bodies. For the dying it must be worse. As soon as death is positive, women's quiet weeping changes into loud wailing interspersed with stereotyped mourning expressions. At the same time the scene takes on a sense of urgency, for there are many things to be arranged immediately even under a cloud of deep mourning. Someone not of the immediate household, often a female neighbor or distant relative, prepares the body by cleaning and dressing it, binding the arms and legs, and placing coins on closed eyelids.[16] Members of the family, usually elder male members, must make arrangements for a burial space in the crowded graveyard, order a casket to be delivered within a few hours, and hire a band to begin playing soon after the body is laid out. Women make preparations for the

---

[14]The majority of native curers are women. The only male curer known to me personally, although informants knew of others, rarely if ever treated people but specialized in curing solares. All informants denied that curers or curing rites were employed for animals, but I learned of one case of a mestizo in El Centro hiring a curer for his dog.

[15]Most drugs, as well as hypodermic equipment, can be purchased without prescription. A few practical nurses specialize in giving shots for a small fee, so that people can obtain antibiotics and have them administered intravenously without consulting a medical doctor.

[16]Informants disagree as to whether or not corpses are bathed.

many accoutrements of death—the great beeswax candles, flowers, river sand, items of clothing, a white sheet for a shroud, incense, and a new *petate* (sleeping mat). Prayer leaders and women to supervise the preparation of food must be contacted and given orders, and the priest must be hired to give the funeral mass. In some households the place where the person died and everything in contact with the person at the time of death is placed in quarantine for eight days, locked up or otherwise isolated to contain the calor of the dead and render it harmless.

Men in mourning wear an armband of black satin while women and girls immediately don total mourning (all black), which includes covering the head with a black cloth or rebozo and keeping it covered for eight days. A large bow of black satin is fashioned and hung over the outside entrance to the solar to announce the death to passersby. This sign of mourning is never removed. Faded to a ghostly gray and whipped by the relentless windblown sand, it will ultimately hang in shreds as a reminder of the household's period of sadness. The condition of the black satin over the entrance is a reliable indicator of the length of time since a death last occurred in the house. Elaborateness and cost of the burial clothing vary with the economic condition of the family. Persons of both sexes are dressed for burial mostly in black, the men with white shirts and black trousers. A poor woman will probably be dressed in a mourning costume she has worn while living; a more affluent woman in a new and costly outfit of black lace or black velvet with white lace *olan* (skirt ruffle) and *huipil grande* (headdress). Sometimes the deceased herself has made a number of funeral preparations in advance such as having her burial clothing made to order, purchasing the shroud, and ordering the candles made, as Doña Rufina did while I was living in her solar.

Once the corpse is prepared, it is placed on a folded mat over a bed of clean river sand on the floor of the house, feet pointing toward and in close proximity to the santa mesa. Two adobe bricks are placed under the head of the deceased as a pillow and two or three white handkerchiefs are unfolded and placed over the face. The 3-foot-tall candles of beeswax and vases of fresh flowers flank the corpse at whose head a little dish containing cornmeal and another with burning incense are placed.

The formal mourning ritual begins as soon as the corpse is placed before the santa mesa. Women gather behind the corpse, facing the santa mesa, kneeling on mats while the *rezadora* leads the prayer chants and an elderly man carefully and profusely incenses all around the body and the santa mesa with smouldering copal incense. These prayer sessions, or *rosarios,* will be repeated continuously until burial, each lasting about half an hour. The women of the household are expected to spend most of these long hours on their knees in the prayer sessions, but they rest from time to time by sitting on a bench. At the end of each rosario women pay their limosna to the female head of the household as they leave. For men and children, mourning is much less strenuous. Male members enter to pay their respects from time to time, kneel and say a prayer before the santa mesa, but they are mainly occupied in the enramada near the men's santa mesa to receive male neighbors, compadres, relatives who pay their cuotas and are given a mourning toast of mezcal or anise-flavored liquor. Children are not much restrained and may go about freely observing all the activities.

A baby or an ill household member may be taken to the solar of a relative or neighbor when a death in their household is near to avoid exposure to the harmful calor.

Musicians, who sit in the enramada, sometimes play from death until burial in the intervals between the rosarios. At other times they are hired to play only at the time of burial, beginning shortly before the corpse is taken to the church.[17] The tropical climate and absence of embalming make burial within 24 hours almost mandatory. If there is a few hours' delay pending arrival of close relatives from distant places, the corpse will be removed from its sand bed and placed on a mat over blocks of ice. The time of the burial is conditioned by hour of death. If death occurs in the hours before dawn, burial will probably take place by 4 P.M. of the same day. At the appropriate time the corpse will be lifted from its bed of sand and placed in the casket, then carried to the church for mass, and then borne to the cemetery, which by law must be a considerable distance from the church. In San Juan Evangelista the cemetery is over a mile from the main church. Even if vehicles are available, the burial procession always proceeds on foot, with two or three extra pallbearers to relieve the six regulars at intervals. Sometimes close women relatives do not go to the cemetery but continue mourning at the rosarios before the santa mesa where the bed of sand remains during the eight days of the novena, either shaped into the form of a cross or left in the approximate outline of the corpse, and covered with fresh flowers and petals. At the graveside a short prayer session takes place, then mourners participate in throwing the first bits of earth on the casket in the grave.

When the burial party returns from the cemetery, a meal awaits them and other mourners regardless of the hour. This meal takes on some of the characteristics of a fiesta as the women chat and gossip and the men imbibe in their corner of the enramada before and after the meal. Men sometimes relate humorous stories, probably in a deliberate attempt on the part of guests to turn the mourning family's attention from the death and relieve the sadness of the occasion.

The rosarios continue every evening for eight days in the solar of the deceased, with neighbors, friends, and relatives joining the family. Early in the morning of the ninth day the household members and perhaps a few family and kin outside the immediate household gather the sand, dry flower remains, fresh flowers, candles, and the two head bricks and walk to the cemetery where the bricks are placed at the head of the new grave and the sand is sprinkled over the surface and covered with the dry and fresh flowers. At death the spirit of the deceased did not immediately reach its final destination but journeyed for eight days, the reason for the eight-day period of intense mourning and prayer.[18]

The river sand and the head bricks have soaked up the sins of the deceased while

[17]When the musicians arrive and how long they play are conditioned by family finances. If money is no object, two or three bands may be hired to provide almost continuous music from the time the body is laid out until after the post-burial meal. Death in a truly destitute family may be entirely without music. I know of only one such case, the adult crippled son of a widow.

[18]Some informants claim the spirit of the deceased lingers around the solar for eight days to see if the family is honoring it properly. Others state that it travels for eight days on a hazardous journey. A spirit which is discontent for some reason—a quarrel with someone or an unfulfilled vow to a saint, or because death was violent and accidental—may linger on the premises for weeks or return later to haunt relatives. Therefore, much care goes in to performing the rituals properly and making the rites as opulent and lavish as circumstances allow.

Funeral Procession, Women's Section (1982)

the corpse lay in contact with them and are purified by the novena rites. The general body of beliefs about death is part of a Mesoamerican pattern deriving in part from the indigenous pre-Contact religions and in part from sixteenth-century Catholicism.

During the forty days following a death, the women of the mourning household leave the solar as infrequently as possible. Selling in the market place is taboo although purchasing is permitted. Men, on the other hand, are free to take up their occupation immediately if they so desire and at most remain in the solar for a day or two after burial of the deceased. At the end of forty days the first and most important mixa gue´tu´ is held, terminating the period of intense mourning.[19] This ritual consists of hiring a priest (sometimes two or three) to say a memorial mass at the church in honor of the deceased, after which relatives and invited guests gather in the mourning family's solar for a ritual meal.[20] A guest list of 200 or more is not unusual, but there is great variation, the smallest affair having only two or three dozen invited guests.

The Wearing of Mourning by Women

The observant visitor to el Istmo will probably note that a great many women and girls are dressed in black. This is not necessarily a reflection of an extraordinarily high mortality rate but of the wide circle of kin and fictive kin for which mourning is worn and the length of the mourning period. For parents women

[19]If the funeral fiesta has been elaborate, the 40-day mixa gue´tu´ may be small, and vice versa.

[20]*Fiesta*, as the term is used throughout this case study, refers to a ritual activity such as a meal or series of rituals activities. It is not necessarily a joyous occasion.

wear full mourning at least one year and semi-mourning usually another year.[21] There is no limit to the extension of the mourning period if the mourner desires. Widows, especially those past middle age, often wear mourning for the remainder of their lives. Grandparents and siblings usually command at least six months' full morning and six months of semi-mourning, and women generally wear full mourning for six months to one year for compadres who were padrinos to their children. Besides genuine attitudes of respect toward the deceased, the fear of censure through gossip assures that an appropriately lengthy mourning period will be observed. Women feel that they make a sacrifice by wearing mourning because it is uncomfortable, unattractive, and usually requires more washing than regular clothing.

In addition, the woman or girl in mourning is supposed to act properly sad and subdued and cannot attend fiestas or other public events. It is not unusual for a woman to be in mourning for several years at a time as one elder relative after another succumbs. Unmarried girls find mourning frustrating, especially for aged great-uncles and great-aunts or padrinos, during the years the girls are searching for husbands. In such cases the girl's complaints will probably persuade her mother to shorten the mourning period. Sometimes a woman will take a vow to observe some additional mourning rite for a certain period of time for a husband or parent. An informant vowed to wear a black head cloth for the first six months after her mother's death in addition to regular full mourning.

After the first mixa gue´tu´ usually two more rites are celebrated during the first year after death. There will be an open house in the solar on *Todos Santos*, November 2, when offerings will be made to the deceased at the santa mesa and at the grave.[22] Then the first anniversary of the death is observed with another mixa gue´tu´ similar to the one at 40 days but often more elaborate. The formal mourning period ends with the first anniversary fiesta, but the anniversary date may be marked on the third and seventh anniversaries by additional mixa gue´tu´.

In summary, Isthmus Zapotec culture is heavily laced with rituals and activities centering around the dead. One might view these practices as ancestor worship since the most elaborated death rituals are for parents and elders. The deaths of small children require simpler and more private family rites while newborn and stillborn infants are usually buried without public ritual.

---

[21]Full mourning is all black, semi-mourning is either black or navy blue with small, simple decorative touches permitted, especially skirts of small white figures on black or navy background, and blue instead of black ribbons in the hair.

[22]Contrary to the custom in Mesoamerica generally, Todos Santos is not a day when every household honors the dead by making offerings in the cemetery. Some do this but it is mainly those households where a death has occurred within the past year. The general time of honoring all dead ancestors is the Easter season for the Isthmus Zapotecs. In San Juan the Thursday before Easter is customary. In San Jacinto Ash Wednesday is observed in one cemetery and Palm Sunday in the other. These are times when literally every family goes to the graves of its deceased kin with food for the living as well as the dead, spending the entire night in the cemetery. A temporary market springs to life in front of the cemeteries where all kinds of food, drink, flowers, everything for the living or the dead is sold. There is music and visiting. It is not a joyous time nor is it especially mournful.

6 / Religion and Ritual

After Contact there developed in many indigenous communities of Mesoamerica a system whereby religious and local political offices were combined and arranged in a hierarchical order, each office in the hierarchy becoming more expensive, with the fiestas for the patron saints at the top of the system. Prestige attached to the offices, or *cargos,* according to each cargo's place in the hierarchy. Usually the cargos were for terms of one year. Although civil and religious offices now must be separate by Mexican law, there are a few indigenous communities where the old civil–religious cargo system continues to function much as it has since colonial times.[1] In most places, however, changes in the system have been profound, sometimes to the point of extinction. In el Istmo there exists today a full calendar of fiestas that are still sponsored by voluntary cargo-holders. Some of the Isthmus fiestas have their origins in the colonial system while others are of more recent origin.

The nature of the fiestas ranges from those that are still considered to be primarily sacred rituals to completely secularized events for entertainment purposes. All are called "fiestas" except the masses for the dead and the attendant ritual meals. San Juan Evangelista is a community in which parts of the cargo system continue to be important as means of achieving and maintaining status and prestige, although the character of the system is changing from an emphasis on public, community-centered fiestas to private, household-centered ones concerned with marriage and death rites. Political and religious offices have long been separated here, the former now elective and appointive, the latter voluntary. In order to distinguish the present system as it exists in San Juan Evangelista from the older cargo system, I shall refer to it as the fiesta system, in which death rites are included.[2]

In the following pages emphasis is placed on the meaning of the fiestas to the participants in terms of social status and prestige. Description of the events of the fiestas will be of minor concern.

Community-Centered Fiestas

The public, community-centered fiestas, on which the old cargo system was built, centered around religious duties and honoring the patron saints. In early

[1]See Cancian (1965) for an account of a cargo system that still maintains its functional integrity.

[2]"Fiesta system" as employed herein refers to a ceremonial or ritual system. Secular fiestas are not included and indeed are still absent in San Juan, although they are the prevalent types in some parts of El Centro and in some other towns of the Isthmus.

Fiesta Procession, Women's Section (1975)

colonial times Catholic padres supervised the construction of churches and cathedrals, each dedicated to a particular saint (or saints) who served as its patron. A sizable town would have a cathedral, whose patron saint was the patron of the entire community, and a series of churches, often one in each barrio, again each with its patron saint representing that particular barrio or neighborhood. Usually, the town and the barrio were referred to by the name of the patron saint, or the older name was retained and the saint's name added to distinguish communities with the same patron saint.

The traditional public fiestas of the Isthmus Zapotecs were noted for their length and elaborateness. In general, they consisted of a series of events covering five or six days, each beginning with a public procession through the pueblo by the *mayordomos* (sponsors), and others directly connected with the events of that particular day and ending in a *vela*, a festival which included music, dancing, and food and drink in the home of the mayordomos. Most public fiestas included a *Convite de Flores* (translated as "reunion of the flowers"), a procession of men and boys in oxcarts laden with flowers, banana leaves, palm leaves, and often an entire banana plant, the oxen themselves decorated with collars of flowers and leaves.[3] The procession of oxcarts ended in front of the church, where the carts were emptied of their contents in a wild chaos of men, oxen, carts, music, and fireworks. Another fiesta event was the *Tirada de Frutas* (throwing the fruit), usually occurring late Saturday afternoon. This began with a procession of unmarried girls in their finest hand-embroidered trajes and gold jewelry parading through the streets with *jicalpextles* (painted gourd containers) of fruit on their heads. The procession ended at the church where the girls either climbed up through the belfry of the church and emerged on the roof or climbed to a platform erected for them in the churchyard. From there they threw the fruit, piece by piece, including heavy papayas, pineapples, and coconuts, and small favors such as paper flags and novelties, into the crowd of children and young men waiting below. Sunday marked the mass in honor of the patron saint and the last day of the fiesta proper. Monday was a special fiesta for the women who had worked preparing and serving the food throughout the long fiesta. This was called the *Lavado de Ollas* or washing the pots but there is little indication that any great quantity of pots was actually washed. Usually this was a daytime fiesta attended almost entirely by women but not limited to the workers only. It was the only occasion when it was permissible for women to drink to the point of inebriation.

The velas, each with a name which was often that of an animal, began in the late afternoon each day of the fiesta and continued to the small hours of the morning, sometimes until sunrise. Each year different households were chosen to sponsor the velas, each household a separate vela. San Juan Evangelista's "Fiesta Titular" had five velas of which only the first is still performed. Older informants remember the sequence of the velas and their names, although all five have not been performed since the early 1940s.

Today, the fiestas in San Juan still incorporate the Convite de Flores, the Sunday mass, the Tirada de Frutas, and the Lavado de Ollas, as well as a procession each day and a *baile* several afternoons and evenings. High prestige still accrues to those households who volunteer to act as mayordomos. Sometimes there is only one sponsor for the entire fiesta, sometimes there are two or three households which share the burden, each sponsoring a particular day's events. In 1967 a committee sponsored one of the public fiestas (the pueblo has two patron saints) through donations from citizens and various fund-raising devices, and the other fiesta had three mayordomos. Acting as mayordomo can still be a large and costly affair requiring the sponsors to burden themselves with heavy debts for several years afterward.[4] Therefore, sponsorship is not undertaken lightly or frequently.

Many ritual acts, including sponsorship of fiestas by individuals or households, represent the fulfillment of a *promesa* made to a saint during a personal or familial crisis. For example, if a child is near death, the parents may vow to a saint that if the child recovers, they will sponsor a fiesta in honor of the saint as payment for his divine intervention. If the child recovers, the parents must make good on their

---

[3]Formerly, sugar cane played a substantial role in the Convite de Flores.
[4]Mayordomos of a public fiesta in 1965 spent about $18,000 of which approximately $7,000 was contributed by others. Compare this to the daily wage of a farm laborer at that time, $10, or the cost of building a first-class traditional dwelling, $20,000.

promise, although it may take years to accumulate enough wealth to do so. Of course, if the parents were poor, with no hope of ever accumulating that amount, they would make a lesser promesa, one whose fulfillment was possible while still representing a substantial sacrifice. The kinds of promesas that are made and the cost of fulfilling them, both financially and in personal effort or discomfort, range from acting as mayordomos or undertaking long pilgrimages to the shrine of a particular saint to simple acts such as burning candles to a saint daily for a certain period of time. Highest prestige is accorded those who sponsor public fiestas to the patron saints because this is seen as a benefit to the entire community; that is, they are paying the expenses so that the entire community can honor the patron saint.

I have stated that households sponsor fiestas. Normally the man and his wife, the household heads, are referred to as the mayordomos. The role of each sex is so vital that if a man is unmarried, his mother, sister, or other close female relative will be chosen to act as his partner mayordoma. Or if the household has no male head, the woman acts as the mayordoma and chooses a close male relative to fill the role of mayordomo. In this case, the fiesta will be said to have had a mayordoma rather than a mayordomo, and the honor and prestige will accrue to the mayordoma and her household rather than to the person whom she chooses for mayordomo. Such cases are not unusual, although fewer women sponsor fiestas alone than couples simply because households without male heads are relatively rare, especially those able to sponsor such a costly event.

Today only a small percent of households in San Juan is willing or able to sponsor public fiestas, even in return for the attendant high prestige and status. Alternate routes to status are becoming acceptable, while some "progressives" actually speak out against the public fiestas as great wastes of money and effort. But many people, especially those not quite wealthy but affluent and upwardly oriented, firmly believe that the mayordomo route is the only acceptable means of establishing a high status for the household.

Family-Centered Fiestas

Most of San Juan's nearly 1200 households can never hope to sponsor a public fiesta, but there are still many ways households can add to their status and prestige through the fiesta system. They can host family-centered fiestas such as weddings and mixa gue´tu´, act as padrinos at baptisms, communions, and weddings, participate as invited guests at the fiestas of others, and make voluntary contributions even if not invited. Each of the four classes or degrees of participation involves expenses and reciprocal obligations.

Hosting Family-Centered Fiestas   Acting as hosts at private fiestas does not involve the fulfillment of a promesa to a saint, nor does the houshold have much choice about when they will give private fiestas involving deaths and marriages. Therefore, prestige does not accrue so much for hosting a private fiesta as it does for "making a good showing" at those the household must give—i.e, by inviting many guests and having quantities of good food, drink, and music. A large private fiesta can be as costly as sponsoring a public fiesta, although that is the exception.[5]

[5]See footnote 4. The most elaborate wedding in many years cost the novio's father something over $20,000 in 1967.

Status Through Compadrazgo   Another prestige-gaining activity is that of sponsorship of children at baptism, communions, and marriage. In order of prestige, sponsorship at baptisms and at marriages is greatest while sponsorship at communions is of minor importance. Sponsoring a child's baptism involves buying the baby's baptismal gown, a candle, and perhaps some memento such as gold earrings for a girl, and paying the church's fee of $10. Altogether, a baptism in 1967 cost the sponsor not more than about $200 initially. Acting as padrinos of a marriage entails a greater cash outlay—for buying or renting the bridal gown and accessories and sponsoring and paying for a part of the wedding fiesta—averaging a total of $1,000 for a "nice" but not opulent wedding. The obligations incurred at the time of sponsorship are only the beginning of the padrino's (or *madrina's*) obligation to the child or couple and their parents. Each of these acts establishes a lifelong ritual kinship between the padrinos and their *ahijados* (godchildren) and between the padrinos and the parents of the ahijados, who become compadres to each other. For this reason, compadrazgo carries much prestige to the sponsoring couple but is limited by their capacity to fulfill the obligations of a growing number of such relationships. Most parents in San Juan choose for their children padrinos who are socially equal or a little better than themselves and who are also residents of the pueblo but are not close relatives. From this clue one may correctly deduce that the people of San Juan think it is most important to enlarge and strengthen their social relationships within their own community and among more or less social equals. This is not to say that compadrazgo ties are never established outside the pueblo or between socially unequal households, but both occur infrequently.[6] Informants were unanimous in stating that the sponsoring compadres occupy the most prestigious end of the relationship and that the parents of the sponsored children as well as the children themselves always owe the padrinos respect and gratitude for accepting such an obligation. Sponsorship is neither asked nor accepted lightly. An average couple will act as padrinos only two or three times in a lifetime; a poor couple with many children, perhaps once or never, while a prosperous couple may eventually establish a dozen or more compadre couples through sponsorship.

Participation in Fiestas as Invited Guests   Invitations to private fiestas are normally extended to a wide circle of real kin, to all *compadres* of the hosts, to persons the host "owe" by reason of previous invitations, and to persons with whom the hosts wish to establish reciprocal relations in the future. The more status the household possesses, the more often will the couple who heads it be invited to fiestas of others, and the more fiestas to which the couple is invited (and attends) the more their status is enhanced. Wedding fiestas include two groups of invited guests, those of the hosts and those of the padrinos, both approximately equal in status. Invited guests are almost always married adults or widowed elderly and most invited guests at any particular fiesta will be elders, individuals who have spent many years incurring and paying ritual obligations in the fiesta system.

---

[6] The compadrazgo system, so much a part of Latin American culture, can be utilized in various ways to strengthen and extend particular types of social relations—between biological kin, between families of unequal social status, between distant trading partners, between non-kin of equal status, and other ways. See Mintz and Wolf (1950) for a concise analysis of compadrazgo.

Invited guests must contribute a suitable amount to the hosts, $3 or $5 for women and $5 to $10 for men, but close kin who are able to do so and compadres are expected to contribute considerably more cash plus a certain amount of food and services. At all fiestas the public paying of cash contributions is one of the most important ritual acts. Men pay their contributions at a table presided over by a president, secretary, and treasurer appointed for the occasion. The religious nature of this act is clear from the name given the men's table—*santa mesa*—which is the same term as for the household shrine. The president greets each contributor formally, the secretary records his contribution, and the treasurer collects and guards the receipts. Another office is that of the toast pourer, a duty which may be shared by two or more men alternately. At the end of the santa mesa is a series of two or more long benches on which the men guests sit after paying their cuotas. The host sits at the head of the bench, next to the santa mesa, usually followed by his close kin and compadres. Each contribution initiates a round of mezcal toasts and cigarette smoking in honor of the contributor.

Women pay their contributions, *limosna*, at the women's table which is usually not referred to as a santa mesa and may not be a table but a large basket or bowl placed on the floor or table, and is presided over usually by only one woman. Each woman receives a toast of sweet wine or grape juice and a cigarette when she makes her contribution. She wears the cigarette behind her ear throughout the fiesta as a symbol of having paid her contribution. At some fiestas she also has the opportunity to buy a paper flower for an extra peso or two which she wears tucked in her hair behind her other ear. All invited women guests do not drink the women's toast at every contribution but are served perhaps two or three times during the course of the fiesta. Women drink beer more or less continuously during the fiesta, but this is not done ritually as with the wine.[7] At some fiestas limosna is recorded, and at others it is not.

It is not uncommon for a woman to make a contribution at the men's santa mesa for an absent or deceased husband. At such time the men toast the absent man with mezcal while the woman acting on his behalf is served the women's sweet wine. I never observed a man making a contribution for a woman at the women's table. In cases known to me, a woman who was invited but unable to attend sent her contribution with a daughter before the event or with a friend or kinswoman who was also invited.

A couple attending a fiesta as invited guests must spend a minimum of $8, often considerably more, but it is not imperative for both to attend. The household's honor will be upheld equally whether one or both attend, the wife making a contribution for the absent husband and thus getting their name on the list of contributors. Women admitted that if they simply did not have the cash, they sometimes invented an excuse and "forgot" to send their contribution, but this was apparently done only in exceptional circumstances. If these lapses of memory were very frequent, gossip would probably result and the houshold's name would begin to appear less frequently among invited guests. At public fiestas and at weddings the total amounts of cuotas and of limosna are announced separately over the public address system at the end of the fiesta, followed by a round of applause.

---

[7]Respectable Isthmus Zapotec women do not drink beer outside of ritual occasions or at home and never drink mezcal or other strong alcohol.

Participation in Fiestas as Voluntary Contributor   The last category of participants in fiestas is that of voluntary contributor. These almost always outnumber invited guests at family fiestas. Any person, even a complete stranger, is welcome to enter a fiesta, make a contribution, recieve the toast or gift and depart. If the donor is a man, he pays at the men's santa mesa, received the cigarette and mezcal and has his name entered in the ledger before he leaves. Because many more women and girls than men make voluntary contributions, there is often a special place set aside for them near the kitchen or back entrance. There, two or three women will be in charge of accepting contributions and giving the contributor some food, typically a small clay bowl of *mole* (thick sauce) with two or three warm tortillas placed on top. This is also given to invited women guests when they leave the fiesta. The usual voluntary contribution is $3 for women and $5 for men, but sometimes several choices are offered to women, the amount of food given varying accordingly. In addition, special items are sometimes sold to pay certain costs. For example, at one mixa gue´tu´ I attended, women who contributed $3 received one *torta* (roll), one chocolate tablet, and a small bowl of mole. For $5 they received double that amount. Sprigs of *cordoncillo* (aromatic herb) could be purchased separately for 50 centavos, the proceeds going to pay for grinding the maize for tortillas.

Households make great effort to contribute voluntarily to every fiesta in their neighborhood plus as many others as possible farther afield. Women make the greatest majority of voluntary contributions on behalf of their household, probably because the man of the house is occupied in his fields or at his trade unless he is an invited guest. If several fiestas happen to occur within a short time, voluntary contributions can strain the resources of a poor household severely. For whatever reason, it often happens that a particular household has no cash at all at the moment it is needed; for example, at the death of a neighbor. In such cases the woman of the household will use every resource she has to get a few pesos together for the contribution. Perhaps she can sell a hen or a small piglet or pawn her earrings. Or she may have a sister or a comadre from whom she can borrow for a few days. The reason ritual contributions are so important is not difficult to understand considering the facts of life and death in San Juan. Every household must meet ritual expenses some time, often unexpectedly when resources are low. Very rarely is there any steady source of income such as wages or salary. The people respond to this "culture of insecurity" with their own mutual-aid mechanism in the form of cuotas and limosnas. One household's ritual contribution to another will be reciprocated on a similar occasion later. Every ritual contribution, voluntary or otherwise, represents either the payment or the prepayment of ritual obligations past or future in an ongoing system in which a balance is never struck.

But it is more than simple economic expediency that motivates people to make voluntary ritual contributions. Perhaps more importantly, contributions are a means of maintaining the household's status in the community. People who cooperate, who contribute as often as possible, even the poorest, will be spoken of as *buena gente* (fine people) while households who refuse to participate or participate with obvious reluctance will be ostracized. "No corresponde," Juanecos say of such persons. "When he dies, there will be no one to carry him to the cemetery." To

Isthmus Zapotecs who value so highly the security of kinsmen and neighbors a worse fate would be difficult to imagine.

The proportion of expenses paid by contributions varies widely according to the type of fiesta and the status and resources of the sponsoring household. Records were obtained from several households which included all types of contributions from relatives, compadres, invited guests, and volunteer contributors. Contributions paid nearly 40 percent of the total expenses of a public fiesta, 35 percent of a mixa gue´tu´, and 20 percent of a very elaborate wedding given by a wealthy household. One informant reported that contributions financed the entire burial and mixa gue´tu´ for her mother because, as she explained, "We have contributed to almost everyone in the pueblo at some time. Many people owed us."

OTHER RELIGIOUS EXPERIENCES

There exist, in addition to those related to the fiesta system, many other possibilities for making and fulfilling vows to the saints. This is a characteristic of Latin American folk Catholicism and is not unique to San Juan Evangelista, yet it is so much a part of the everyday lives of the people that the discussion of religion and ritual would not be complete without reference to it. Zapotecs also often make vows to honor ancestors. For example, a friend vowed to honor her deceased mother by going to a church in another community every month for one year on the anniversary of her mother's death. Making and fulfilling small vows is so common that people rarely mention them. It is the rare, perhaps once in a lifetime, fulfillment of vows which informants recount with pride. Among these are pilgrimages to the shrine at Esquipulas, Guatemala, more than a thousand miles away. Formerly it was undertaken on foot and horseback, all persons from the pueblo with a vow making the trip together. The pilgrimage took almost three months and entailed great hardships and dangers. Older people recall how everyone left at home rejoiced when the pilgrims finally returned safely. Now the trip can be made by rail and bus in a week to ten days. Fewer persons go each year than formerly. Another popular pilgrimage is to Astata, only eight or ten hours by *redila* (stock truck) but still a hazardous journey because of primitive mountain roads. Astata is the site of miraculous rocks that are said to drip the blood of a saint and to produce water as long as a candle is kept burning in honor of the saint. Several informants had made this trip to fulfill vows, although women sometimes go primarily to sell at the fair rather than for religious purposes.

Another means of fulfilling vows involves building a chapel in honor of the saint. The several chapels that dot San Juan all originated this way, the newest built at the entrance to the cemetery only a few years ago by a young matron, the nature of whose vow I neglected to learn. The construction of such a chapel in honor of a saint is considered a community service because it brings the saint's blessings to the whole community just as do celebrations in honor of the patron saints.

SUMMARY

In summing up the fiesta system as it exists today in San Juan Evangelista, it is apparent that sponsoring public fiestas is still an important means of gaining the

Todos Santos Offering, Household Shrine (1990)

highest respect of the community. Hosting private fiestas also adds to status and prestige, especially when food, drink, and music are abundantly supplied. Sponsoring baptisms and weddings is another status-enhancing activity. All these separate acts are cumulative in their effects on the household's status. Persons who are most frequently invited to fiestas are the gray-haired elders who have made countless ritual contributions, have sponsored baptisms and marriages, have hosted family fiestas, and perhaps have acted as mayordomos or anticipate doing so in the future. In effect, such persons have lived a life of service to their community for which they receive the honor and respect of their neighbors and status and prestige increasing through time. A household need not accumulate wealth to gain respect. The ideal is rather to share one's wealth for the benefit of the community, the ancestors, and the saints.

Anthropologists have often explained the widespread Latin American fiesta system as a leveling device, a way of insuring that community solidarity is not threatened by great differences in wealth. Development agencies have most often viewed the system as a block to capital accumulation and subsequent investment in capital-producing goods on which economic development depends. Both are correct when the system is viewed from afar. Yet it is important to remember that to the people within the system it is the social ties which the fiesta system establishes and maintains that give life meaning.

Nonetheless, indications are that in San Juan as elsewhere the fiesta system is losing ground. It is deprecated by members of the mestizo culture as wasteful and senseless, views which are presented to school children. Men now rarely cooperate to provide the necessary labor of erecting the enramada, slaughtering the animals, and other heavy tasks of fiestas. This labor must be paid nowadays. The women continue their cooperative labor and their enthusiasm perhaps because for the women the fiesta system remains one of the most important aspects of life, almost the only diversion in a life of hard work and monotonous routine, something to look forward to in the later periods of life when the cumulative effects of participation in the system will have enhanced one's status and prestige. This is not to say that the fiesta system has lost its meaning for the men. They still participate along with the womenfolk on behalf of their households, although their cooperative labor has virtually disappeared. Still most of them, except the very old and the most traditional, seem less enthusiastic than the women.

In 1967 it seemed to me that the fiesta system was on the wane and would

Women Distributing Fiesta Food (1975)

probably die out. In 1990 that seems less imminent, if not unlikely. The system has changed, to be sure. There is now more emphasis on the life-crisis rites as means for gaining family prestige, a change that has been noted elsewhere in Mexico by Stephen (1990) and others, while the public ceremonies to patron saints continue toward secularization and co-optation by political entities. In 1990 a split between the younger, more educated, salaried families and the traditional, little-educated families is becoming apparent as well. The latter continue to support the old system enthusiastically while the former wish to spend their surplus on conspicuous consumption as a means to prestige, viewing the ritual expenditures as a waste of resources and, therefore, undertaking them with reluctance. Since there is still a very large number of traditional families in San Juan, it seems probable that they will keep the fiesta system alive for at least another generation or two.

7 / Social Relations in Nonritual Contexts

Conceptualizing the Isthmus Zapotec social system in terms of an overlay map, each successive layer representing a level of the social system, we have exposed and examined several layers in previous chapters. The preceding chapter described the prevalent behavior patterns and types of social relations associated with religious rituals. The present chapter is concerned with two overlays or levels simultaneously: social relations in secular contexts and the underlying beliefs and attitudes that form the bases of behavior in such non-religious contexts.

We have learned in the previous chapter that the people of San Juan Evangelista come together in large groups in the fiesta system and cooperate to accomplish a particular goal, whether it be honoring the patron saint, celebrating a marriage, or paying homage to the dead. Particularly noteworthy is the fact that such large, cooperating, face-to-face groups organized for a common purpose occur almost wholly in religious contexts. Without the sanctions of religion the people seem unable or unwilling to cooperate in large face-to-face groups to accomplish some purpose. There are no voluntary associations such as economic cooperatives, unions, parent–teacher associations, fraternal orders, service clubs, and others so familiar to North Americans. A few associations that exist of necessity "on paper" seldom if ever meet as a group. Suspicion and secrecy permeate secular social relations. Physical aggression and even violence are expected from neighbor and stranger alike; the universe is perceived as filled with threats and dangers. Fear, one discovers, is a dominant emotion in San Juan. People *express* many specific fears—of strangers, of the unknown road, of wild creatures supposed to inhabit the mountains, of being alone, of illness, of ghosts, of envy and anger, of thieves and burglars, of bats, and of witches.[1] The list is far too lengthy to summarize here. Unexpected fears, an equally long list, manifest themselves in people's behavior— fear of conflict, of political involvement, of falling victim to the perfidy of a friend, of betrayal of a confidence, for example.

Clearly, the people of San Juan view their environment, indeed their whole universe, as essentially threatening and dangerous. Why? In terms of Isthmus Zapotec peasant culture, I think their view is not unrealistic. Given the general state of insecurity and the more or less continuous threat of real disaster which hovers

---

[1] I had a quite undeserved reputation for valor which rested mainly on the fact that I had driven a pickup truck all the way from California to San Juan alone and that I lived alone during the first ten months of fieldwork. As to living alone, what people mistook for courage was actually more a result of circumstances and an inadequate understanding of the culture. I would not repeat that mistake.

over people's lives in the form of destitution, illness, and death, people's fears simply express their anxieties over the uncertainties that face them daily. Add to these real threats the body of beliefs and attitudes concerning causes of illness, death, and other misfortunes, and something that might be called a "culture of insecurity" emerges.[2] Behavior that at first seems irrational, even paranoid, to the outsider begins to make sense in the context of the Isthmus Zapotec social system.

Of course, people in every society face some degree of uncertainty in life. In peasant communities generally, as in San Juan, the level of insecurity is many times greater than it is in our own society because people live much closer to an absolute subsistence level than most of us can imagine. In such a community what would be a small adversity for ourselves can be a disaster. Because of the general low level of health and sanitation, illness can be very serious, frequently fatal. One's land and possessions can disappear through treachery, legal maneuvers, and thievery, one's assets can be quickly dissipated in medicine, drugs, medical doctor's fees and the more modest fees of native curers. Insecurity, then, centers around loss of health, life, and property. The causes as well as the agents of misfortune may be natural or supernatural. For example, the arousal of envy in a neighbor can bring misfortune and disaster to a household in various forms. The envious person may injure through actual physical aggression or he may work through supernatural means such as witchcraft and spell-casting. The prudent individual protects himself and his household from envy and other threats to security in many ways. First, he tries to avoid arousing envy by his own actions and behavior. Second, he tries to protect and fortify his household in order to limit the danger of physical aggression. Third, he protects himself and his household by supernatural means through the use of protective and preventive magic.

BEHAVIOR TO AVOID AROUSING ENVY

The wise person avoids arousing envy by taking certain precautions. She conceals possessions from the eyes of outsiders, neighbor and stranger alike. The mother covers the baby from harmful admiring glances, some of which may be open expressions of envy.[3] Gifts and purchases other than food are transported in covered receptacles or otherwise hidden from curious, perhaps envious, eyes. Any accumulation of goods or improvement in the household's circumstances is kept secret as long as possible. One cannot live long beside the main entrance to the pueblo without becoming aware of a considerable traffic by foot, by oxcart, by truck and taxicab, entering and leaving San Juan in the hours between midnight and dawn. At first I assumed that people merely wished to take advantage of the cooler temperature to move goods, begin long journeys, or begin preparations for early

[2]Foster (1965) explains many similar behavioral characteristics in Tzintzuntzan and other peasant communities as responses to a particular cognitive orientation which he terms "The Image of Limited Good." Foster's model fits the Isthmus Zapotec data well and could be used. However, the real threats and the perceived threats in San Juan seem to me to be both adequate and more directly explanatory of behavior in the specific context of Isthmus Zapotec culture.

[3]There are other reasons for shielding babies. In addition to envy, ojo may result from even a person of goodwill if they do not counteract the admiration with a pat on the head or buttocks of the child. Susto can also result from the baby being frightened by unfamiliar persons or objects.

market transactions. All of these reasons are valid on some occasions, but a major reason, secrecy, escaped my attention for months. Only when I was making arrangements to move from a rented house into Doña Rufina's solar did the importance of secrecy become apparent.

The paucity and humbleness of my possessions by North American standards was such that I had considered myself to be living very simply with the barest essentials. The furniture consisted mainly of rough shelving for books and storage and two work tables made locally of low-grade unfinished lumber, a portable typewriter, tape recorder, an old card table and a couple of ragged and rusty canvas lawn chairs. The heaviest moving task involved a dozen or so cartons of books, field notes, office supplies and papers. I did not anticipate that the move would require more than hiring a couple of porters for perhaps two hours. I asked Doña Rufina what would be a convenient time for moving. "Well, I've been thinking about that," she replied. "I think you should just bring one thing over here each night after dark. No one will realize you are moving all your things in here." I protested that the move would take too long. "But if people see you bringing all those things into my solar they are going to be envious of me," she said. I argued that everyone knew the furnishings were mine, not hers, so there would be no reason for people to envy her. But Doña Rufina was not convinced. "Take my advice. I have lived in this solar so many years (nearly forty) without trouble because I have always been cautious. *!Fijate!* All those years I sold maize from my solar nobody knew how much I sold because I always had the carretas (carts) of maize delivered at night. When we built this house, I accumulated the bricks cartload by cartload for years, and nobody knew what we were about because everything was brought in at night. I kept the building supplies hidden over in that corner beyond the big rock until we had almost enough to complete the house." But in the end, after considerable discussion, Doña Rufina agreed that I might move in over the course of three or four evenings without arousing too much attention.

The examples cited by Doña Rufina are some of the kinds of precautions people take to avoid envy. There are many others. If one wishes to accomplish something or make a purchase which can be expected to arouse envy, a great deal of advance planning, maneuvering, and consideration of possible alternatives may be involved. In one case an informant wanted to buy *cebu* cattle as an investment. Government agencies have tried to encourage the breeding of these animals in preference to the criollos, but in San Juan cebus in 1967 were still uncommon, partly because they were costly animals. My informant, Jorge, considered the alternate plans of buying the herd one animal at a time over a period of months, of buying the whole herd of twelve animals at one time and donating two of them to the saint's herd to "show people I am buena gente," and of buying only six young calves at first "to see what happens." In the course of six or seven months during which Jorge considered the best approach, there were probably other possible courses of action considered and forgotten by Jorge during the intervals between our occasional conversations. Finally Jorge purchased two cebu calves and used the rest of his savings to buy a herd of criollos from a relative because in this way nobody would realize that the criollos had changed owners and the two small cebus would be scarcely noticed.[4]

[4]Cattle are pastured on communal lands. In this case the purchased herd remained in the same area it had been previously, only the owner and the caretaker changing.

SECURING THE SOLAR

One of the best protections against acts of physical aggression, whatever the cause, is a secure solar. In San Juan the more prosperous the household, the more secure will be the solar for two reasons. Making a solar impervious to intruders is costly, and the prosperous household provides the most tempting target to would-be thieves as well as being most vulnerable to envy. A secure solar is enclosed on all sides by an 8- to 10-foot high adobe wall, often with jagged broken glass cemented into the top. There is a single opening to the street which can be securely barred. In modern solares, the door may be metal instead of wood. Window openings will be covered with iron grillwork and closable from the inside by wooden shutters. Glass windowpanes are avoided since they present an irresistible temptation to rock-wielders. If there is an unshuttered window which opens onto the street, one must be careful not to sleep or place a sleeping child near it, even in the daytime. It is too easy for any passerby to toss a rock or bottle through the opening. Also, precautions must be taken to keep objects inside the room far enough from the window so that they cannot be reached from the street by long arms. All possessions, including maize, mangoes, coconuts, bananas, or other products brought in from the fields must be stored within the solar. The only animals more or less immune to theft are dogs and cats. Cattle thefts in el monte occur with such regularity that people view the losses as calculated risks of owning cattle. Even growing crops are not safe from thieves and vandalism.[5] Physical aggression that may be caused by envy or anger or simply an easy target is usually attributed to males and seems most often to be directed toward other males, in part because the socialization of girls includes actions and behavior designed to avoid and discourage aggression. Not infrequently, physical aggression expresses itself in homicide, which may spark a series of reprisals.

Supernaturally caused misfortunes are especially feared because the agent that brings them may be as elusive as a will-o'-the-wisp, and cure is impossible until the agent is identified. Therefore, a household can be rapidly impoverished to the point of destitution while seeking the causes and trying various cures for a series of misfortunes or a lingering illness. Again, prevention through one's own actions is the wisest procedure. Supernatural causes are discovered only *post facto*. That is to say some misfortune, usually illness, occurs. It does not respond to the usual simple treatments of curers, medicines, perhaps the efforts of a medical doctor, or certainly nowadays, injections of antibiotics. The first curer called will have divined a cause before treatment and acted accordingly. Probably other curers will be called in succession, each of whom will divine a cause and treat the patient for a time. This can continue until the patient is cured or the family's patience or resources are exhausted. Witchcraft may be cured by stronger countermagic. The diviner cautions the client not to reveal the identity of the witch lest she (or he) invoke more powerful magic against the victim. Other supernatural agents include spirits of the dead. One who dies violently may linger around the cemetery for years, frightening passersby, pursuing them through the streets at night, and playing the usual ghostly tricks. Quarrels and conflicts between persons might cause the spirit of the one who

[5]Celso found several rows of a small patch of sorgo cut and removed by thieves shortly before it was ready to harvest. This field was about four miles from the pueblo.

first dies to plague the other. The best protection is to be especially careful to observe all the death rituals with proper respect so that the spirit will be content to forget the earlier conflict. Even when there has been no conflict, deceased kin can cause trouble for the living. Perhaps a promesa was left unfulfilled or the spirit may simply be reluctant to leave her home and her loved ones. Who knows what spirits of the dead may do? Again, proper attention to death rituals is the best insurance against later complications.

If supernatural causes are only discovered after the fact, the threat is constantly present. Any unfamiliar person who behaves suspiciously, an animal that acts strangely, and even an unfamiliar discarded object tossed carelessly in front of one's door can be causes for alarm.[6] Again, preventive measures and precautions are wise. The curandera is called when there is a possibility that one has been exposed to supernatural forces.

Women are thought to be witches more often than are men, maybe because witches are also usually curers and there are many more women curers than men. Women also employ native curers for themselves and their children many times more frequently than do men. As an informant stated, "We [women] use curanderas a lot because we have so much trouble [illness]." Contrary to reports from some other Mesoamerican peasant communities, the witch may be a close neighbor to the victim.[7] Conflicts are avoided between the victim and the witch because the latter's identity must remain a closely guarded secret between the diviner and the victim. But even if one's neighbor is not known to be a witch, a chance remark overheard can be interpreted as an evil wish. For example, an informant's 12-year-old son became ill and remained so despite every effort to cure him, including consulting medical doctors, who diagnosed the trouble as a kidney ailment. After several months the boy's condition seemed actually to be deteriorating. One day the mother overheard her neighbor remark to a visitor that it appeared the boy might die. The mother was deeply disturbed, interpreting the comment as a wish that the boy would die. She immediately began to think of her neighbor as the possible cause of the son's illness, although of course this was not revealed to the neighbor.

One's own strong emotions can also be dangerous. A person can die from his own anger, and suppressed anger can be as lethal as anger expressed. It is easy to understand why people fear situations in which differences of opinion and conflicts might arise. Illness and death caused by anger arising within the victim is referred to as *coraje*, while illness caused by fright is referred to as *susto* and *espanto*.[8]

---

[6]During mango season when I was selling mangoes with informants in the Oaxaca market place, a mestizo woman loitered around among the vendors most of one day trying to entice young women to "go to work for me in Mexico," offering to pay $1,000 per month. The work was supposed to be care for an invalid son, but by her actions I guessed she might be connected with some illegal activity such as prostitution. The girls avoided her because her behavior indicated to them that she was a witch.

[7]In some Mesoamerican peasant communities witches are reported to always be identified as someone living at the opposite end of the pueblo. Such identification may serve the same purpose as keeping the witch's identity secret in San Juan—to avoid open accusations and overt hostility. One of my informants was employing a curer in 1967 who had been identified as responsible for some family illness several years earlier. The illness was later found to be caused by the spirit of the deceased household head, after which it was cured. Of course, the curandera was not aware that she had been suspected of witchcraft previously.

[8]In some places susto and espanto are distinguished. Susto is usually caused by a real fright while espanto is an illness caused by some supernatural agent. In San Juan the two are used interchangeably.

One avoids frightening or startling another person. Even a small child in San Juan knows better than to sneak up behind his friend and cover the other's eyes with his hands. That would be an intentional attempt to cause susto. To avoid sudden fright, people try to make their presence known when one's back is turned or something prevents one from hearing another's approach. On one occasion I was startled by my closest friend while typing. She was so upset that she almost wept for fear that she had given me susto, explaining that she had called and thought I had answered.

Admiring glances directed toward women and children, whether or not the admirer's intentions are friendly, can give rise to illness. The admirer may be of either sex but the admired are almost always women and children because "we are more attractive and others are jealous," an informant explained. Therefore, small children are kept in the solar out of sight of admiring glances.[9] People who "know how to act" may admire the baby openly because they counteract any possible harm from ojo by patting the child's head or buttocks. Attractive women may have trouble all their lives, which require the frequent employment of curanderas to counteract the ojo. A healthy person is better able to ward off illness whatever the cause, and people clearly understand that a weak body will be more susceptible to serious illness. There is great concern with health and the maintenance of a healthy body, although the preventive and precautionary practices are not the same as those recommended by modern medicine. One protects her health by trying to maintain a balance between the effects of hot and cold on the body's humors, a concept that derives from Hippocratic medicine via sixteenth-century Spain and remains to this day widespread in Latin America. If a person has a fever he does not aggravate it by eating or drinking hot substances. One protects himself from the night's chill by not eating or drinking cold substances in the late afternoon.[10] Most fruits are considered cold and avoided in the tardecita (late afternoon) along with other cold foods.

It is not possible in this brief volume to describe in all its rich detail the many threats to health, life, and property and the attendant behavior which is so much a part of day-to-day living in San Juan. Adequate treatment of just this single aspect of Isthmus Zapotec culture would require a volume in itself. I have tried instead to convey to the reader something of the beliefs and attitudes that strongly influence people's behavior and to illustrate that in terms of the beliefs and the conditions of life, the Isthmus Zapotec world is a dangerous and threatening place. It must be stressed that the residents of San Juan are not unique. They share their beliefs and behavior with all Isthmus Zapotecs of similar socioeconomic conditions and to a large extent with all peasant peoples of Mesoamerica. Indeed, some traits described here are found in peasant communities the world over. Nor would it be fair to neglect to mention that some residents of San Juan consider these folk beliefs as superstitions and that many elites in El Centro, not native to the Isthmus, believe in

---

[9]Doña Rufina related of her second daughter: "Amalia was such a beautiful child with her curly hair that we were always having to call the curer for her. Even now that she is many years married and with children she still has trouble."

[10]The identity of a substance as hot or cold is not logical in our terms. Ice, for example, is a "hot" substance. Those foods identified as either hot or cold vary somewhat among informants and also there is variation between San Juan and other parts of Mesoamerica.

and practice some of this "folk medicine," even though they say it is all superstition believed only by poor, ignorant campesinos. Indeed, I think it would be difficult to live in the Isthmus for any length of time *without* coming to practice and even believe in the efficacy of folk medicine or *without* becoming suspicious, distrustful, and secretive.

There is evidence, not yet substantiated by research, that the Isthmus of Tehuantepec may be the scene of more political unrest and violence than is generally true of Mesoamerica. Again, two conditions may exist in San Juan itself that could enhance the anxiety level. The first concerns land and municipio boundaries about which the people have good reason to feel insecure and threatened (see Chapter 4). The second condition, for which I lack comparative data from other Isthmus communities, is the relatively high level of physical aggression. Some of this occurs among residents of the pueblo to be sure, but a considerable amount of such behavior seems to be directed toward Juanecos by individuals and factions outside the municipio. Whatever the rationalization of Istmeños, I suspect that the old political factionalism continues to be a strong incentive to aggressive acts. San Juan's location, combined with inadequate and almost totally ineffective law enforcement, makes the municipio a haven for criminal elements. In addition, the pueblo may attract acts of vandalism by outsiders simply because chances of apprehension are so small.[11] These conditions may lead the residents of San Juan to feel more vulnerable and insecure than is true for El Istmo in general. While certain groups and individuals in El Centro characterize the people of San Juan as especially aggressive, violent, and barbarian, my research and impressions cannot support such opinions. Acts of physical aggression occur in every Isthmus community and, indeed, in every human community.

SOCIAL RELATIONS IN AN INSECURE ENVIRONMENT

In the first part of the chapter the focus has been on the people's perception of their environment as dangerous and threatening and the precautionary measures that are taken to ward off or reduce the dangers. In this section, social relations are described, beginning with the household, then progressing to the larger kin group, compadrazgo, neighborhood, and community at large.

Social Relations Within the Household

The household is the basic social as well as economic unit, its members closely bound together by ties of kinship, affection, and mutual dependence. It is the most closely knit group in Isthmus Zapotec culture, although the members are not given to open displays of affection except toward small children. As in all human families, sex and relative age are major determinants of roles within the household.

---

[11]This seems to have been true in my case. Several attacks of rock throwing during the night hours culminated in two young men gaining sufficient courage to climb through the window into my sleeping quarters. Fortunately, I awoke and fled. Although I was the target, the cause was probably nothing more than the fact that I was a "gringa" living alone in a house that did not offer sufficient protection. The aggressors were probably not from San Juan.

The eldest able-bodied couple are the acknowledged heads, the man being the official representative of the household in affairs of the community at large, but the wife representing the household in contacts with other women. Ideally, the male elder member of the household is "head of the household." In practice, the husband–wife team forms a strong, egalitarian partnership with much of the actual burden of day-to-day responsibility and decision-making falling on the wife. Since she has been well prepared by a long apprenticeship, first in her mother's household and later in that of her mother-in-law, when she at last heads her own household, it is most often with confidence and efficiency borne of experience and maturity. Dependent, clinging-vine-type wives are so rare in San Juan that I met none at all in interviewing more than 50 wives in a household survey.

Isthmus Zapotec women form the closest affective ties with their children and occupy the central kin positions of the culture. The role of mother overshadows the role of wife, one of the criteria of a matrifocal culture. Deference to husbands by wives is sometimes a polite formality but husbands defer to wives with about the same frequency. Wives name their husbands as household head, more because it is the ideal and expected response than because it reflects reality.

Isthmus Zapotecs conceptualize the mother as the stable, loyal, trustworthy element of family life while father is affectively more distant—first, because he is away from home much of the time and second because, in fact, fathers are not always reliable providers. Isthmus Zapotecs are not unique in Latin America in placing a high value on the role of mother. This theme, which Evelyn Stevens refers to as "marianismo," is widespread in Latin American culture and crosscuts both class and ethnicity. Indeed, the ideology of the moral superiority of women and the

Mother and Daughter in the Countryside (1967)

almost sacred role of mother, so prominent in Latin American Catholicism and largely absent in Old World Catholicism, may well have derived from the pre-Contact egalitarian social structures and religions of the New World.

San Juan residents state that women should (and do) handle household money because "the man might get drunk and spend it all in one night but mothers always think about how they are going to feed their children." Heavy drinking by men is a fact of every religious festival, including weddings and funerals, but it is especially demanded by the ubiquitous festivals to the patron saints. At any of these affairs a man might well consume a liter or two of mezcal in mandatory toasts over the course of a few hours. This pattern of ceremonial alcohol consumption leads a number of men into chronic alcoholism by middle age. In addition to drinking, men's reputation as unreliable providers derives from the not infrequent abandonment of families by fathers who too often take up with another woman and create a new family to the economic and emotional detriment of the first.

An essential function of the Isthmus Zapotec household is mutual protection. The male role centers around actual physical protection while female roles are more concerned with protecting the health of the household members through proper preventive and curative measures. Previously it was noted that Zapotecs do not enjoy solitude and never live alone by preference. The more household members, the more secure is the household from physical acts of aggression. A person left alone by death or circumstances can usually "borrow" grandchildren, nieces, nephews, or more distant relatives to live in the solar, or can close the solar and move into the home of kin. The household without an adult male in residence becomes more vulnerable to vandalism, burglary, and theft than would otherwise be the case. Nonetheless, circumstances often force elderly sisters or a mother and daughter to live alone. Doña Rufina related that when she and her 12-year-old daughter lived alone in the solar for some months after her husband's death, they were so frightened that they huddled together at night in a single hammock, trembling at every unfamiliar sound. Most of the solar was secured by metal doors with locks but the back part where cooking was done had only a reed fence. Doña Rufina painted a broad white stripe on the house wall there where it would be visible to an intruder. She thought the stripe would frighten an intruder who would mistake it in the darkness for a man. The stripe was still doing sentry duty ten years later during my residence in her solar. A few months after Doña Rufina's husband died, her youngest daughter fell ill. In the process of discovering the cause of the illness and trying various cures, Doña Rufina had the solar cured and thereafter she felt more secure.[12]

As noted earlier, the poorer the household the less secure it will be because locks, iron grillwork, and metal doors, as well as high adobe walls, are costly. On the other hand, the poor household does not feel as threatened in terms of thieves and burglars because of its poverty. "Who would be so foolish as to think we had anything of value?" or "We are just poor simple people with nothing to fear," people may say, but this is only relatively true. An informant, Rosita, and her

---

[12]Curing a solar involves hiring a curandero who comes at midnight and places magical substances, including a pair of *chiles anchos*, in previously prepared holes in the floor and walls of the solar, the latter near entrances and openings. During this process, the curandero is chanting prayers. The holes are then sealed over so that they cannot be easily detected. Curing a solar is a closely guarded secret because the protection is only effective if nobody outside the household has knowledge of it.

husband lived in a very small solar without modern conveniences. The floor of the little house was of packed earth, the two window openings had been filled with loose adobes against a time when they might be able to install grillwork and shutters, the solar was enclosed with only a reed fence and closed with a rickety reed gate that had to be propped shut with a pole. Usually this childless couple felt moderately secure from intruders because they had nothing of value in the solar, but when they temporarily had to store maize, sesame, or mangoes after harvest one of them had to remain in the solar at all times until the produce was sold and delivered. "If I am not right here," said Rosita, "the *mazorca* (ear corn) will just walk away."

The household, then, offers physical security from outside threats as well as emotional and economic security to its members. Anyone who lives alone, as I did for a time, and lives alone by preference, is completely beyond comprehension. A person without kin is to be pitied. When I was introduced to someone for the first time it was always with the explanation that "she is all alone, far from her family."

Social Relations with Kin Outside the Household

The bilateral kinship system and prevalence of community endogamy (that is, most marriage partners are natives of San Juan) mean that a great many households in the community are related to each other by kinship and marriage. But the pattern of emigration, which is of long standing, and patrilocal residence also have the effect of widening the kinship circle to include families in distant places, especially in Mexico City and the state of Veracruz. The kindred, that group of persons which each individual recognizes as his kin, never functions as a unit, although portions of the group cooperate on ritual occasions. In day-to-day living, kin ties outside the household may, but do not always, take precedence over those with nonkin. Most persons are on friendly terms with part of their kindred, indifferent or even hostile to others. The Isthmus Zapotec ideal is that social relations between siblings will always be close and cordial throughout life, and that kinship itself, whatever the degree, should always be marked by mutual trust and cooperation. Those ideals are seldom realized.

After siblings reach adulthood and marry, close relations between them may continue or may cool to the point of noncommunication. Conflicts among adult siblings often seem to arise over matters of inheritance. Among the five separate families of adult siblings with which I was most familiar only one, consisting of three sisters, was not divided. In three of the other four families, conflicts and alienation were of long duration. In the fourth, the disagreements were recent and possibly would later be resolved. Adult children may even quarrel with their aged parents over favoritism shown to siblings, although respect for parents seems usually to prevent complete alienation.[13] Adult siblings who remain on friendly terms provide mutual assistance and protection to one another beyond what can be expected of any other kin outside the household, and it remains probably the closest relationship beyond the household unit.

[13]Indications are that respect for and responsibility toward aging parents by adult children may be changing, aided by the national courts. In a recent case (1990), parents and six other adult siblings brought suit against one daughter who was not paying her share of support for the parents. The parents and siblings lost the case.

Social Relations with Compadres

The compadre relationship, as noted previously, is primarily a formal, as opposed to familiar, one. Still, it is very important in terms of mutual security, providing a relationship *de confianza* second only to real kin.[14] Once established, the compadre relationship ideally remains active throughout the lives of the persons involved, binding the households of compadres into a reciprocal supportive relationship resembling that expected of true kin. Compadres owe one another moral and financial support in times of crises and on ritual occasions. Padrinos (referring to couples) are usually called in to arbitrate marital problems or family conflicts among adult siblings after parents die. However, the nature of Isthmus Zapotec social relations is such that some compadre relations also break down. Sometimes there is a complete break and the two couples involved simply cease to recognize the existence of the relationship. More often the relationship gradually becomes inactive over time unless it is reaffirmed at frequent intervals through reciprocal behavior—courtesies, gifts, invitations, and favors. In other words, for the compadre relationship to remain effective both couples must consciously work to reaffirm it. This is easier when both couples live in the same community and are more or less social equals. Perhaps this is the main reason the people of San Juan prefer to establish compadre relationships within their own community and social class. The few compadre relationships established outside tend to be mainly inactive unless there is frequent contact, such as between women vendors occupying adjacent stalls in the market place.

Social Relations Among Neighbors

The people of San Juan seem very urbanized in their attitude toward nonkin neighbors in that they prefer to keep a certain degree of social distance while remaining on neighborly terms. Because adjoining solares often have only reed walls separating them (although the ideal is adobe), privacy between neighbors can be a problem in small solares. Mainly neighbors support one another in ritual contributions, especially those involving deaths. Women neighbors seem to cooperate in small, informal ways more than men but that may be simply because women have more need to exchange services and spend more time in the home. Certainly it would be much more difficult for a woman to live on unfriendly terms with her neighbors than it would for her husband who is usually away during the day.

Among neighbors, then, there is little intimacy or genuine supportive friendship unless kinship is also involved, but one can usually count on neighbors for help in times of mutual threat such as to chase away intruders or to protect the solares from fire, floods, and other natural disasters and on ritual occasions and mutually beneficial economic transactions.

---

[14]Berta, a middle-aged widow, was comadre to Rosalia by virtue of having sponsored Rosalia's daughter at baptism. When the child was about six years old, Berta became her aunt as well as her madrina by marrying Rosalia's brother. There was some discussion between the comadres, now sisters-in-law, about whether the daughter should continue referring to Berta as madrina or should begin calling her *tia* (aunt). Rosalia suggested that tia was more appropriate because kin relationships, even affinal ones, are closer and more intimate than fictive kin relationships.

Social Relations in the Community

In the first pages of this chapter, the absence of secular voluntary associations was noted. The people of San Juan, therefore, do not meet in groups to make community decisions. This is especially apparent when one discovers that those organizations or associations that do exist on paper by virtue of necessity seldom if ever meet.[15] Instead, the group's business is conducted on a dyadic basis. When compared to our own culture, Isthmus Zapotec preference for dyadic relationships, those involving only two persons or couples, is striking.[16] This means that if a group decision must be reached or a certain amount of consensus is necessary, concerned individuals will discuss the matter privately on a dyadic basis with those other members with which they have amicable relationships. This amounts to sort of an informal poll-taking to assess support or opposition by the few individuals most interested in the subject under discussion. Action will finally be taken along the lines indicated by the majority of the members unless the dissenting minority has rather pronounced objections, in which case a split into strongly antagonistic opposing factions may occur, thus preventing the taking of any constructive action whatever.

Since organized opposition can paralyze decision-making, very commonly individuals in charge try to make unilateral decisions covertly. These often lead to *post facto* conflicts, of course, but the more unilateral decisions that can be made and the fewer of these that become public knowledge, the better the chance of some action being taken on behalf of the group, whether or not it is the best or preferred action of the group as a whole.

When leadership is in doubt, that part of the community that might reasonably be counted on for support can be polled on a dyadic basis, while those individuals who might be opposed may be "inadvertently" bypassed. During 1966–1967 there was some effort to crystallize opinions by circulating petitions among household heads—to sign if they favored the proposed action. As a hypothetical example, if an individual was dissatisfied with certain actions or inactions of the pueblo's presidente, the dissatisfied individual could circulate a petition stating his case and asking for signatures of persons in favor of relieving the presidente of his office. Naturally, the complainant would contact first those households where he could count on support, while trying to muster as many signatures as possible before the presidente and his friends learned of the petition. The presidente's supporters would then begin circulating a counter petition. Eventually each side would have a petition with the signatures of those household heads on which they could count for support. How successful the circulating of petitions has been is uncertain. A number of informants claimed they never signed petitions because it was too easy to become embroiled in controversy. There is a feeling that committing oneself to any side of a conflict is dangerous and can lead to disastrous consequences. Signing a petition

[15]An example is the association of *ganaderos* (cattlemen) to which every cattle owner belongs by virtue of owning animals. No cattle can change ownership without a certification of ownership by the seller through this association.

[16]The preference for dyadic relationships is widespread in peasant communities in Mesoamerica and other parts of the world. See, especially, Foster (1961), "The Dyadic Contract: A Model for the Social Structure of a Peasant Village." Foster's model and aspects of it have been employed by a number of anthropologists.

commits the signer unequivocally, whereas verbal commitments can be more easily denied. Perhaps indicative of people's attitudes toward petitions was the story making the rounds, probably untrue, of a local politico who was embarrassed to discover he had signed petitions of two opposing factions.

It is apparent that community action outside a religious context is very difficult to achieve. This might be one of the reasons that the cargo system evolved in the colonial period through which local political and religious offices and duties were bound together. In San Juan, at any rate, the absence of religious sanctions in community affairs effectively forestalls cooperation and community decision-making and leads people to distrust local leadership and one another.[17]

SUMMARY

While household ties are the closest, followed by close kin outside the household, then compadres, none of these relationships, except that of mother and children, seems to be as close and binding in real life as the cultural ideals prescribe. For all their emphasis on never being alone, Isthmus Zapotecs tend to be lonely individuals, even within the household unit, never completely trusting even the most trusted of kin. They seem to be continually searching for social relationships in which they can place trust and continually anticipating disappointment. Kin become alienated; compadres do not respond when such is their obligation; neighbors are spiteful and envious instead of friendly and cooperative as they should be. Every social relationship seems to be less enduring and less intimate than is desired. The individual longs for loyalty, friendship, and security, yet expects to be betrayed. People speak of being *celoso* (jealous) not in terms of sexual jealousy but in terms of friendship and loyalty. Velia tells her comadre she is jealous because she saw her talking to another woman. She expects an explanation and a reaffirmation of the close comadre relationship, such as: "Ay, comadre, it was nothing. She is only an acquaintance, a friend of my sister. She cannot take the place of my comadre." But Velia is not completely convinced.

An atmosphere of real insecurity thus leads the people of San Juan to feel threatened by real and imagined dangers. Insecurity feeds back upon itself, creating more and more protective, distrustful, suspicious behavior, until the entire social system is permeated with anxiety and paranoia. Cooperation in ritual contexts thus becomes important as a reaffirmation of faith in one's fellows and in social relations generally.

[17]In 1990 there are encouraging signs that more community cooperation is occurring, a subject dealt with in more detail in the final pages of this volume.

8 / Isthmus Zapotec Matrifocality

MATRIFOCALITY AS A CULTURE TYPE

The term *matrifocal culture* does not appear in the first edition of this volume because the concept of entire cultures being matrifocal, as opposed to an occasional aberrant family within a culture, had not yet been proposed. It was not until 1974, when Nancy Tanner's article "Matrifocality in Indonesia and Africa and Among Black Americans" appeared, that I realized that Isthmus Zapotec culture represented a classic case of the type of culture she described as being matrifocal.

Earlier social scientists had recognized that some cultures and subcultures produced a number of matrifocal families, but these were seen as aberrant family types caused by the absence of a father figure and a result of extreme poverty in urban environments, especially among urban Blacks in the United States. Nobody had recognized that there are cultures that subscribe to the legitimacy of matrifocality, that do not view it, as we here in the United States have, as a "breakdown" of the patriarchal family.

Tanner's definition of a matrifocal culture includes the following four criteria:

1. The role of mother is "structurally, culturally, and affectively central," and such centrality is viewed as legitimate." (Tanner, p. 131)
2. The relationship between the sexes is relatively egalitarian.
3. Both women and men have important economic and ritual roles.
4. Girls are socialized to become assertive, active, and decisive wives and mothers.

Let us consider the first criterion briefly in the context of Isthmus Zapotec culture. The mother would be structurally central to the family probably everywhere in the world but she is not always *culturally central*. Cultural centrality requires that the people hold an *ideal* of the mother role as central to the functioning whole of the culture. Historically, the mother in the United States has not been culturally central although the mother role has long been romanticized by politicians, theologians, and others for their own purposes. The cultures of New Guinea and the Middle East come to mind as other examples of cultures where the mother is *not* central to the functioning of the culture as a whole. Over the world there are probably more cultures where the mother is not culturally central than otherwise, although there seem to be differing degrees of mother centrality from culture to culture.

"Affectively central" refers to the intensity of emotional ties. If emotional ties between mother and children are the strongest in the family and that is viewed as proper, then the mother can be considered as affectively central. The United States has a considerable history of vituperative literature by social scientists and others

The Author's Compadres (1967)

condemning the "overly affectionate, overly protective" mother as damaging to her children, so while the mother may in fact be affectively central, many people, including the "experts" have not viewed such a role as proper.

Legitimacy refers to what members of the culture consider to be correct—the expected behavior. Matrifocality in our culture has no legitimacy because it is seen as an aberrant, dysfunctional family form that sometimes occurs but should not be encouraged. In contrast, Isthmus Zapotecs view the centrality of the mother role as "the way things should be."

As emphasized throughout this case study, Zapotec women hold strong roles economically, socially, and in the kinship system. The father is almost always living in the Zapotec matrifocal household, and relations between husband and wife tend to be highly egalitarian. It is not only *acceptable* for women to exercise power and authority in their everyday lives, it is culturally expected and encouraged.

Matrifocality, although comparatively rare, has been reported in widely scattered and very distinct culture areas around the world. Tanner includes as examples the Igbo, a patrilineal, patrilocal culture of West Africa, the Javanese (bilateral kinship and neolocal residence), the Atjehnese (bilateral kinship with matrilocal residence), and the Minangkabau (matrilineal, matrilocal), the latter three Asian. The Isthmus Zapotecs have bilateral kinship and patrilocal residence. This variety of kinship systems indicates that there is no necessary connection between kinship type and matrifocality. Although at least some of the Afro-Caribbean cultures possibly could be described as culturally matrifocal, on mainland Latin America only the Garifuna of Belize have been so described (Gonzalez, 1970, 1984; Kerns, 1983). A point deserving special emphasis is that the sexes in matrifocal cultures have more or less equal status, each sex having its own spheres of action and influence. Cultural matrifocality in no way implies weak, subordinate status or attenuated roles for men, nor does such occur anywhere.

MATRIFOCALITY AND WOMEN'S ROLES

It was in an attempt to explain the elusive quality of relationships between the sexes that has led casual observers to characterize the Isthmus Zapotec social system as a matriarchy that I first developed the model of Isthmus Zapotec gender roles described in the following pages. Popular stereotypes based on romantic fantasies to the contrary, anthropologists have never documented a matriarchal society anywhere in the world. Indeed, the picture I have drawn in the earlier chapters of this volume more accurately describes a patriarchy. But neither of these extremes alone conveys to the reader that blend of Isthmus Zapotec gender roles which leads to a fine balance of equality between the sexes. As previously noted, matrifocality (in contrast to matriarchy) can function perfectly well along with a patriarchal superstructure because matrifocality operates mainly at an informal level and often in separate arenas from the patriarchal overlay of male roles. The gender role model represents the final stratum of the hypothetical cultural overlay map introduced at the beginning of the case study

A MODEL OF GENDER ROLES

If one thinks of the social system as made up of roles (defined earlier as bundles of rights and obligations), one might compare a social system to an iceberg. What has been described to this point is the visible part of the iceberg—the part that includes the formalized roles. A large part of the Isthmus Zapotec social system, like the iceberg, is submerged and invisible. The submerged part of the social system, the nonformalized roles, is as crucial to an understanding of Isthmus

Zapotec culture as is the visible part, the formalized roles. Furthermore, it is in this submerged part of the system that the roles of women are so important.

Formalized and Nonformalized Roles

Formalized roles are here defined as those given formal status and recognition by the members of the society. That is, every adult member of the society recognizes the existence of the role and has a fairly clear concept of the rights and obligations the role demands, even though he may never be expected to fill the role. Examples might be the roles of mother, father, or presidente of the municipio.

Nonformalized roles are those that are not so clearly perceived or rigidly defined by the members of the society. Most people may not be aware that the role exists, and even persons filling such nonformalized roles may perceive their own behavior as individual action without structure or pattern in the larger system. Only the observer becomes aware eventually that nonformalized roles exist, an awareness occasioned by observing repeated instances of similar behavior by many different individuals in many different contexts. A number of examples of nonformalized roles will be presented later in this chapter.

Anthropologists and sociologists are probably uncomfortable with nonformalized roles even when they are well aware of their existence. The reason for this discomfort may lie in the lack of effective research tools for investigating such roles systematically and the absence of models for integrating them into descriptions of social systems. If the nonformalized roles are powerful, there has probably been some attempt to incorporate them into description, often in an unsystematic way just as they occur in the field notes, leaving the reader to draw her own conclusions as to how to integrate them into the social system. Some attempts have been made to explain nonformalized roles by presenting the formalized roles as the social system and then adding data concerning nonformalized roles as "exceptions to the rules." A few more sophisticated attempts to deal with nonformalized roles will receive fuller treatment in following pages.

Public and Private Domains

A role model of Isthmus Zapotec society is presented in Figure 8.1, with roles divided along a horizontal plane into formalized and nonformalized categories and along a vertical plane as existing in private or public domains. The private domain refers to the family or domestic group, while the public domain refers to the remainder of the social system. The rectangle in Figure 8.1 represents the totality of roles that make up the social system, with Line A separating formalized and nonformalized roles and Line B separating private and public domains. The level of Line A is arbitrarily drawn to the degree that incomplete and inferential data indicate that nonformalized roles probably predominate in Isthmus Zapotec culture. They may be more or less prevalent than Line A indicates. On the basis of the wide range of variability known to exist in other aspects of social systems crossculturally, I would hypothesize that Line A might be drawn either considerably higher or considerably lower for any other specific social system.

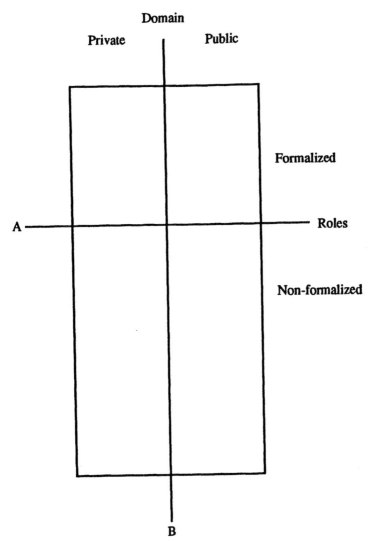

Figure 8.1. A Model of Roles in the San Juan Evangelista Social System

The Sexes and Role Type

Although we can only guess at the adaptive significance of assignment of certain roles by sex or the evolutionary processes involved in such assignment, a universal fact of human societies in which public and private roles are differentiated is that men have traditionally filled most of the formalized roles in the public domain. Furthermore, in many societies, perhaps most, men also fill, in the private domain, those formalized roles that require regular interaction with male roles in the public domain. An example is the role of father as head of the family, which will normally include his acting as intermediary between the family (private domain) and the outside world (public domain), especially but not exclusively where the role in the public domain is held by a man. This function of the male head of the family is very apparent in San Juan, as it is in our own social system as well.

Some roles in the public domain form complementary pairs by sex. An example would be the President and First Lady of the United States or the fiesta sponsor and his wife in San Juan. However, complementary pairs seem to be few in the public domain in most social systems. In the private domain, on the other hand, they abound. Mother–father, husband–wife, sister–brother are all complementary pairs of roles, as is that of parent-child, the latter assigned on the basis of relative age rather than sex.

Universal Role Assignment by Sex

In every society, women's formalized roles in the private domain include the major responsibility for rearing children in the early years of life. Nearly universally, the role of the woman includes preparation of food for male adult family members as well as for children and the majority of domestic tasks in and near the house site.[1] As previously noted, among the domestic roles of men are those that require interaction or possible contact with persons in formalized roles in the public domain. In addition, men's roles in the private domain center around making and maintaining the technology required for the man's subsistence activities and his maintenance of order within, and protection of, the private domain.

Harris summarizes universal roles assigned by sex as follows (1971, pp. 581–582):

1. In all hunting and gathering societies men specialize in hunting the large, dangerous, migratory, and swift game, while women specialize in small game, shellfish, and vegetable products.

2. In all known human societies men have exercized the dominant role in the maintenance of law and order in nondomestic contexts, especially in intergroup relations. (Matriarchy has never existed.)

3. In all known societies, the primary police-military force consists of males specially trained to use fighting weapons. Females are seldom trained to use such weapons.

4. In all societies, women are the specialists in rearing infants.

Roles and the "Status of Women"

In every human society status is assigned to formalized roles. Status is that degree of value or prestige that the society attaches to a particular role as compared to other roles. As a rule, formalized roles in the public domain seem to be almost always more important in conferring status than those in the private domain. There is no doubt that nonformalized roles may also confer status and prestige in some cases, as seems to be true for the Isthmus Zapotecs, but it is a difficult task to evaluate nonformalized roles along these lines because of their nature.

It is a truism that the "status of women" in any given society is never higher than that of the men; that is, women as a group are never accorded dominance over men

[1]See Brown (1970).

as a group (Harris' No. 2 above). Where formalized roles occur in complementary pairs by sex, the male role of the pair is usually but not always accorded higher status than the female role. The reasons for such regularities having developed and philosophical arguments about their justification, although intriguing subjects, are beyond the scope of this case study. The higher value placed on men's roles is not necessarily derived from rational considerations. For example, in hunting and gathering societies men's subsistence activities are always the most highly valued, yet women's subsistence activities almost always contribute considerably more than 50 percent of the total food supply of the group (Lee and DeVore, 1968, p. 4; Lee, 1968).

Within the limitations just set forth—that women's roles are never dominant over men's roles in any society—there is, nonetheless, great variation from one society to another in the status of women as a group compared to men—from equal at one pole to grossly unequal at the other pole. On such an imaginary continuum, I would place the Yanomamo of South America as reported by Napoleon Chagnon (1968) and the Tiwi of North Australia as reported by Hart and Pilling (1960) near the low-status pole. The Isthmus Zapotecs would be near the high-status or equal pole. Where our own society in pre-1970 times would have fallen I am not prepared to state, although I perceive it as having been lower than that of the Isthmus Zapotecs.[2] In 1990 I think women's status in the United States has improved enough to perhaps be considered equal to that of Isthmus Zapotec women (equal but not along the same parameters—we *do not* have a matrifocal culture).

On what basis a society determines the status of the sexes is far from clearly understood. We can no longer claim that men's higher status rests on their greater contributions to the subsistence base nor can we state that women's status tends toward the lower end of the hypothetical continuum in simple hunting and gathering societies and toward the opposite pole in modern complex societies, although that has long been a popular ethnocentric assumption. Perhaps status according to sex has much to do with how much importance the society places on sex as a status marker compared to other status markers such as age or social class. There may be some relationship between status by sex and the value the society attaches to nonformalized roles in the public domain. Probably we shall eventually discover that a combination of many variables is involved.

Nonformalized Roles

For the Isthmus Zapotecs, nonformalized roles play a very important part in the social system. But what is meant by nonformalized roles? Eric Wolf speaks of core

---

[2]Before about 1970 when the Women's Movement began, women in the United States had been devalued, denigrated, and discriminated against in every imaginable way quite openly, denied education and job opportunities, paid low wages, deliberately kept out of all-male professions such as medicine, engineering, science, and law and male occupations (which included the bulk of all occupations). But the greatest difference between pre-1970 U.S. and the Isthmus Zapotecs was the degree to which women in the U.S. have been historically ideologically devalued, taught subservience to men, and told daily in countless subtle and nonsubtle ways that they were not as capable or strong in body or mind as their brothers. Younger people may argue with this but they have not experienced pre-1970 America for 45 years as I have. In contrast Isthmus Zapotec women are culturally valued, taught they are beautiful, capable, strong, desirable individuals and taught also to be tough and assertive, to speak out for justice no matter what the consequences.

and periphery structures in complex societies, three of which he designates as kinship, friendship, and patron–client relations. Although he focuses on structure rather than role and does not relate core and peripheral structures to the assignment of role by sex, he seems to have in mind something very similar to what I here call formalized and nonformalized roles. Wolf states (1966, p. 2): "We thus note that the formal framework of economic and political power exists alongside or intermingled with various other kinds of informal structure which are interstitial, supplementary, parallel to it." Others have more explicitly referred to roles and to role assignment by sex. Riegelhaupt (1967), for example, distinguishes between formal and informal roles in a Portuguese village. Ernestine Friedl (1967) makes a similar distinction for Greek peasant society, and Aswad (1967) refers to key and peripheral roles of noblewomen in the Middle East.[3] It is probably not accidental that anthropologists concerned with role types as they relate to women's roles have often been those with research experience in peasant societies. This fact might suggest that nonformalized roles and informal structures are more important adaptive devices for peasants than for some other social types. But perhaps it is premature even to suggest such relationships when we know so little about nonformalized roles and informal structures in various social systems.

Even in simpler social systems one frequently encounters in the ethnographies some reference to what apear to be women's nonformalized roles. The following description of the Tiwi of Northern Australia illustrates women's nonformalized roles in the political domain of a society of hunters–gatherers ruled by a male gerontocracy (Hart and Pilling, 1960, pp. 52–53):

> The "game" was one of trying to win friends and increase prestige and influence over others. . . . The most concrete symbol of Tiwi success was the possession of surplus food, for this not only permitted its possessor to make gifts to others and throw large parties for which he picked up the check, but also gave him lots of leisure time to devote to social and political life. Since a man required a large number of women in his work force if he was to build up a surplus of food, in the final analysis it was control of women that was the most tangible index of power and influence. Women were the main currency of the influence struggle, the main "trumps" in the endless bridge game.
>
> . . . To a smart Tiwi politician, wives or daughters were assets but so was his mother—if submissive to her son's wishes. So were his sisters—if amenable. A bachelor at the age of thirty who had several sisters was a lucky young man, especially if those sisters already had daughters to their current husbands. As successful old men used their infant daughters to gain influence and buy satellites, so young men used their mothers and their sisters—if they could. . . . The devious details of Tiwi prestige and influence operations are much easier to follow if one keeps in mind the crucial fact that the Tiwi men valued women as political capital available for investment in gaining the goodwill of other men more than they were interested in them as sexual partners. . . .
>
> Women were, however, a form of capital that possessed the power of talking back to the investors. As daughters or as wives they were quite thoroughly subordinate to the wishes of their fathers or husbands, and Tiwi wives were as frequently and as brutally beaten by their husbands as wives in any other savage [sic] society. But as mothers and as

---

[3] I owe much to several individuals who have contributed to the formulation of the role model. Riegelhaupt (1967) describes the formal and informal roles among Portuguese peasant women, and these seem to be rather close to my formalized–nonformalized role dichotomy. From Friedl (1967) I have borrowed the terms *public domain* and *private domain* but employ them in a somewhat different manner.

sisters the women were not coerced by their sons and their brothers. On the contrary, sons or brothers wishing to use their mothers or their sisters in their political schemes . . . could only do so with the active collaboration of the women concerned. Tough-minded young widows could drive a hard bargain with their brothers as to where they remarried, since each needed the other to make the remarriage acceptable to the tribe at large and to beat down the other competitors (the dead husband's brother, for example) who wished to control the remarriage of the widows. Young girls had no bargaining power but young widows had a good deal. Old mothers with influential senior sons were extremely powerful. Any affront to an old woman was an affront to her sons, and some of the strongest influence networks were alliances of several senior brothers, in which their old mother seemed to be the mastermind and the senior sons largely the enforcers of what the old mother and her middle-aged daughters (their sisters) had decided among themselves.

. . . Not as independent operators, but as behind-the-scenes allies of their sons and brothers, Tiwi mothers and sisters enjoyed much more essential freedom in their own careers as often-remarried widows than would appear at first sight in a culture which ostensibily treated all women as currency in the political careers of the men. No matter how males, both old and young, might connive, they were constantly aware that no remarriage of a widow could ever be arranged and made to stick unless the widow herself was agreeable.

In the above example, Tiwi women have formalized roles as "currency" in the political games of influence and prestige men play, clearly an inferior, powerless role. *But* mothers and sisters fill powerful nonformalized roles in the same game. This nonformalized political role of certain kin categories of women is not sufficiently pervasive to place Tiwi society very high on our hypothetical status continuum according to Hart and Pilling's account.[4] Women's nonformalized role is viewed by the men, in fact, as a hindrance rather than an aid to their political maneuvers. Perhaps there is some relationship between women's status and whether their nonformalized roles are viewed as complementing or competing with the formalized roles, although I have seen no crosscultural data to support such a suggestion.

Another example of women's nonformalized roles comes from an incident that occurred in a peasant community in Puebla, Mexico, as related by Elmendorf (1971):

Facilities had been arranged for short-term loans which would allow the purchase of hybrid seed and fertilizer, which could easily be repaid from the promised doubled yield of the first crop. The farmers were enthusiastic at the presentation, but none followed through with a request for a loan. Dr. ___ explained that he finally learned from his field workers that the wives were not permitting their husbands to go into debt, and that as soon as the program was presented and explained to the women, loans were taken out.

In the Puebla community, women clearly have an important nonformalized role in economic decision-making in the private domain. A number of other examples could be cited from other sources. Friendship, for instance, could be considered a

[4]Goodale's account of women's roles in *Tiwi Wives* (1970) did not come to my attention until my original case study was already in publication. On the basis of her data I would place the Tiwi somewhat above the Yanomamo (Chagnon) on the hypothetical status of women continuum discussed in the text. Now several of these restudies of previously described cultures have appeared and they all bear the same message. Male anthropologists working through male informants and female anthropologists working mainly through female informants will get very different views of women's roles and status. See Annette Weiner's capable and revealing restudy (1976) of Malinowski's Trobriand Islanders as an example.

The First Woman Elected Official, with Daughers—a New Formalized Role for San Juan Women (1990)

nonformalized role (or in Wolf's terms, part of the informal, interstitial structure) which occurs in most social systems. Friendship may be formalized to a certain degree in some social systems and nonformalized in others. Among the Isthmus Zapotecs, some friendship alliances may eventually evolve into the highly formalized role of compadre, in which case the relation changes from one of friendship to one of fictive kinship and the role changes from nonformalized to formalized.

FORMALIZED ROLES AND ISTHMUS ZAPOTEC WOMEN

An examination of the formalized roles in the Isthmus Zapotec public domain indicates that men and male formalized roles usually carry higher status than women and female formalized roles. The women of San Juan confirm this daily by a hundred different acts and statements. It never occurs to them to resent this order of things. That is simply the way the universe was created. To question woman's status compared to that of man would be as absurd as to question why one must breathe to live. Although in 1967 no woman of San Juan had ever held nor ever expected to hold an office in the *ayuntamiento* (municipal government), I subsequently learned through longer acquaintance with San Juan politics that their mirth at my suggestion of such a possibility had more to do with the common conception that public offices are filled only by persons wishing to "rob from the people." Any politico is considered to be dishonest, and therefore, most men too avoid public office.[5]

There were no women among the 16 or more *xuanas* (headmen) in the ex-distrito of El Centro (which includes San Juan) in 1966–1967. Informants did not recall any woman holding the office in the past although the suggestion appeared to seem less improbable than a woman in the ayuntamiento. The reason could be that Isthmus Zapotec women hold up more than "half the sky" in the religious realm of the system and the office of xuana by 1967 was mainly a ceremonial role.

Women's Recent Semi-Formalized Political Roles

In the 1970s Isthmus Zapotec women, particularly in the large regional market center of San Vicente, began to take a more formalized role in the political protests and upheavals that have wracked the region. There the marketwomen and businesswomen (comerciantes) have been at the forefront of the political disputes over municipal elections. The city made international headlines in 1981 when the local Coalition of Workers, Campesinos, and Students (acronym COCEI), which included many women, supported the Popular Socialist Party (acronym PPS) candidate who subsequently won the election. It was a history-making upset for the dominant Mexican political party, the Institutional Revolutionary Party (acronym PRI), which has controlled the republic for some 60 years.[6]

Campbell (1989) states that women, many of them market women, regularly comprise at least half of the participants in COCEI demonstrations and protests and that the party is heavily dependent on the women's active and militant participation and contributions. He further reports that the women are "consistently among those wounded or jailed during repression" and that several have lost their lives in these violent confrontations with authorities.[7]

[5]The tragedy of this is that honest men have held political office and tried to improve the pueblo but the lack of public trust has always defeated them sooner or later. In the 1989 election an apparently honest and sincere presidente and his slate of lesser officials (including the first San Juan woman to be elected) were voted into office. In 1990 rumors were flying that opposition forces were about to "pull him out of office" because of some purported misconduct, real or imagined.

[6]Howard Campbell (1989, 1990) ably and thoroughly documents this long struggle, including women's roles in it.

[7]Having given this positive picture of women's political participation, Campbell then paradoxically concludes that Isthmus Zapotec culture is not sexually egalitarian because women do not hold formal public political roles, have fewer educational opportunities, are subjected to domestic violence and put in "double days." The same can be stated of our own culture in 1990 and, indeed, of the entire world. The sexual egalitarian measurement I suggested was based on those cultures which are *most nearly* egalitarian in gender roles. No culture has yet achieved true equality for women.

The women of COCEI do not represent a new phenomenon. These semi-formalized roles of women come to the forefront and become more formalized in crisis situations. The reader will recall from earlier pages that Isthmus Zapotec women were active participants in the 1680 insurrections and subsequent uprisings and protests through the centuries. There is ample evidence that their political particpation becomes active and aggressive whenever they feel their homes, their community, and their livelihoods are being compromised by a corrupt male-run political structure. The 1980s have been a severe crisis era all over Mexico, and women have become politically involved in other communities as well. Martin (1990) describes an interesting parallel among mestizo women in a small pueblo in the state of Morelos. In San Juan women have not been as politically active as their neighbors because San Juan is a much smaller community and COCEI members are neither as numerous, nor as strong, nor as ideologically committed.[8] Through 1990, PRI continues to be the party in power in San Juan. Nonetheless, as we shall shortly learn, women fill extremely important nonformalized roles in the political life of San Juan, as important to the continued functioning of the pueblo as are the formalized male roles.

Turning to the fiesta system, one finds that more importance traditionally has been attached to men's formalized role of contributor–participant than the same role when provided by women. Men's contributions are called cuotas (assessments) and are always recorded while women's contributions are designated as limosna (donations) and are often not recorded (although they are remembered nonetheless). Women pay men's cuotas in their absence or even after their death. Men never do this for women's limosnas. Finally, women bear the brunt of the observation of strict mourning taboos. When a death occurs in the family, men and boys may resume their work almost immediately, but even if the family is dependent on a woman's earnings in the market place, custom prevents her from selling there until 40 days have passed. The strength of this sanction is illustrated in the following example.

> Petrona's mother died after a long and costly terminal illness. Petrona had not lived in her mother's solar since her marriage 15 years earlier. When her mother fell ill, Petrona took over the mother's pottery post in the market place to help out. During the illness of more than two years, Petrona contributed part of the earnings from the stall to her mother's expenses. Petrona's older sister, a single viajera, had borne much of the expense and had been forced to stay with her mother so often that she was finding great difficulty making ends meet. When the mother died, income was badly needed to pay off debts and meet current expenses. Two weeks after the mother's death Petrona asked me what I thought about her reopening the pottery puesto. I told her I thought people would understand the situation, knowing the long terminal illness of her mother and the need to meet expenses. Although apprehensive about what people would say, she finally decided to go to the market place if I would stay with her to give her moral support. We opened the puesto at 7 A.M. the next day. None of her market neighbors seemed concerned and her customers expressed no dismay, surprise, or disapproval of her behavior, at least not overtly. Everyone seemed friendly and helpful, but Petrona was so certain that her selling after only two weeks would cause a scandal that by 10 A.M. she had developed a severe

[8]I owe this information to a personal communication from Howard Campbell.

headache. She closed the puesto before noon and did not reopen it until after the 40 day mixa gue´tu´. Her sister, the viajera, also did not leave the solar of her mother until the end of the 40-day period.

NONFORMALIZED ROLES AND ISTHMUS ZAPOTEC WOMEN

Since Isthmus Zapotec women have relatively few powerful formalized roles in the public domain while the female half of complementary role pairs in either the public or private domain is ideally subordinate to the male role, it may seem puzzling that I place Isthmus Zapotec society high on the continuum of women's status. A thorough examination of the nonformalized roles of women should help clarify this apparent contradiction because it is in the nonformalized roles that Isthmus Zapotec women play such a vital part in the social system.

As mentioned previously, violence is an expected male behavior pattern, especially dangerous when the man is intoxicated. Anger is an emotion which is always thought to be perilously close to the surface in the male personality, an emotion which can suddenly flare into violent acts. Women too are capable of anger, but a woman's anger is seen as less apt to result in violence and less threatening to community solidarity, since it is most often confined to the private domain. At least three presumptions about male behavior figure in women's assessment of social situations and the appropriate response either through an individual act or a nonformalized role. First, it is presumed, as stated above, that men will always react aggressively and violently when conflict arises between men. Second, it is presumed that all men will make sexual overtures to any woman, given the opportunity. Third, women presume and fear that a husband will sooner or later wish to establish sexual relationships with one or more other women, perhaps ultimately creating a second family, which will divert already scarce resources from the first family. All such presumptions reflect a certain degree of reality and are shared to some degree by both sexes, but many Zapotec men follow few or none of the presumed patterns. Perhaps the two most important factors that guide behavior in Isthmus Zapotec culture are fear of loss of life, health, and property (as discussed in a previous chapter) and the common presumptions about the nature of men. These two factors may give rise to the necessity and the opportunity for women to function in many nonformalized roles in the public as well as the private domain. In other words, in Isthmus Zapotec society nonformalized roles may be considered an adaptive mechanism, and women thus may have an adaptive advantage, conferred by the total social system, in filling most effectively such nonformalized roles as those described herein.

I do not imply that women fill all nonformalized roles. Men almost certainly also fill a number of important nonformalized roles in Isthmus Zapotec society. The political factions that seem to be endemic in San Juan function largely through male nonformalized roles, for example, although women also play nonformalized roles at times in the same arena. Since I was a woman investigating women's roles, the obvious outcome is a better understanding on my part of women's nonformalized roles.

Nonformalized roles can be used either overtly (with the people affected aware of the role as in friendship) or covertly (with the people affected by the actions unaware of them). In general, overt roles involve behavior that is socially acceptable and acknowledged. Covert roles, while not readily observable, may be merely manipulative or they may be illicit. The nonformalized roles of Isthmus Zapotec women seem most often to be overt or, if covert, used for benevolent manipulative purposes, such as to avert confrontations between men.

Women's Overt Nonformalized Roles

In San Juan the primitive communication system (no telephones, local television coverage, United Parcel Service, or daily newspaper) make the roles of women as messengers and reporters of great importance to the menfolk while the pervasive fears of envy and violence make the roles of women as intermediaries and agents no less essential.[9] In this connection it must be remembered that most men are away from the pueblo during daylight hours six or seven days a week, working in their fields or elsewhere. Furthermore, women's marketing activities allow the movement of women almost anywhere in the pueblo or in El Centro at almost any hour without arousing suspicion while such movements of men would be much more noticeable and, therefore, possibly suspect. As they make their daily excursions to and from the market places and one another's homes on marketing business, women can carry messages mentally and articles not intended for the public eye buried in their baskets. Women usually function as messengers and reporters for the convenience of the menfolk of the household as in the following examples from my field notes:

Case 1: Alvaro has a pair of young oxen to put out on a three-year contract. He has discussed the matter two or three times with Isabel (his wife) and Doña Teresa (his mother). The problem is that he knows of several men who would probably want the toritos, including Jesus (his brother-in-law), who doesn't know Alvaro has the toritos, it seems. Contracting them to Jesus is out because of his binges, during one of which he is reported to have left a team of oxen belonging to Doña Teresa without feed and water for several days. When discovered, they were almost dead, according to Doña T. Alvaro doesn't want to arouse Jesus' envy or add to some already apparent resentment on the part of Jesus. This morning it seems he has solved the problem. He told Isabel to stop by the solar of Apolinar on her way to the plaza to see if they might want the team. I suspect a factor in his decision is the location of Apolinar's fields near Santa Rita, far removed from the fields of Jesus, which would facilitate transfer of the toritos without Jesus' knowledge.

Isabel carried the message as requested. As it turned out, Apolinar did not need the toritos, but it was arranged that the son of one of his compadres should take them. The latter lived at El Jacal, again well removed from the resentful eyes of Jesus. By prearrangement, Apolinar's compadre and his son arrived by truck at the solar of Alvaro a few nights later, signed the contract, and then, accompanied by Alvaro, proceeded to el monte under cover of darkness to pick up the calves.

[9]Several public address systems, located in widely separated parts of the pueblo, charge a fee for each public announcement. Most public announcements concern weddings, fiestas, deaths, elopements, items for sale, and lost-and-found animals.

Case 2: Late this afternoon while I was at Doña R.'s, Inez (her married daughter) arrived unexpectedly to warn José Luis not to be seen with his partner, Victor Manuel F. The rumor is circulating that someone is looking for one of Victor's brothers, who has suddenly disappeared. She doesn't know of the source of the trouble or any details yet.

The background data for the above incident is as follows: José Luis had just recently bought a small herd of cattle in partnership with Victor who was a distant relative. They were not particularly close friends. The partnership had evolved when Victor had encountered a "deal" on a herd in Chahuites (about 100 km. distant) and did not have enough cash to swing it alone. In casting about for a partner he approached José, who happened to have the cash on hand and had, in fact, been considering buying some cattle. When the rumor involving Victor's brother reached Inez' ears, probably no one but the immediate families of the two partners knew that they were in partnership on the cattle. The reasons for Inez' warning and the urgency with which she brought the report can best be understood by following the cattle partnership through to it dissolution two years later. A short time after Inez' warning to her brother, another of Victor's brothers (not the one reported to have disappeared) and a boy passenger in his truck were ambushed and killed on the street in San Juan. Immediately after this unfortunate incident, Victor Manuel left the municipio. José Luis was stuck with the care and expense of the entire herd of cattle, which he could not sell without his partner's signature. About a year later José Luis went north and found employment, turning the management of the cattle over to one of his several sisters, whom he instructed to keep trying to get Victor's address from some of his relatives so that the needed signature could be obtained. Finally, two years after the formation of the cattle partnership, Victor's mother, who had also left San Juan for security reasons, returned for a short visit during which time José's sister and Victor's mother were able to dissolve the partnership by proxy. In this case, the role of women as agents in the cattle partnership was crucial to its successful and eventual dissolution.

Case 3: When Don Guillermo's mother died, I drove him out to the cemetery to arrange with the caretaker for a burial plot. To "do the talking" he chose a young woman relative whom I had not met previously, although there were several male relatives and compadres in his solar at the time. Don G. was incapacitated by profound grief from making his own arrangements since the trip to the cemetery was made within two hours of his mother's death. Don G. wanted his mother buried in one of two spaces next to the chapel, both of which were reserved, according to the caretaker. The agent, Catalina, did all the talking on Don G.'s behalf. After several minutes of bargaining wih the caretaker, she pulled $50 out of the waistband of her skirt and handed it to the caretaker. He said it was not enough, but accepted reluctantly after Catalina reminded him that the burial space was, after all, only temporary. (When the family for whom the space was reserved needed it, Don G.'s mother would be moved, a common practice in San Juan.) Catalina also made arrangements for the grave diggers, and she and I brought to the cemetery and served the meal to which they were entitled when finished.

Several months later an occasion arose during which I could ask Don Guillermo why he had chosen Catalina, who was about 30 and a very attractive woman, to make arrangements at the cemetery. He replied that bargaining with a pretty woman makes it difficult to answer in the negative. But, as I later learned, Catalina's husband's family was well-to-do and Catalina herself had inherited a respectable sum of money, both of which contributed to her status. There were probably ties of some sort (patron–client, landlord–renter, compadre, other) between the cemetery caretaker and someone in Catalina's family or that of her husband which made it even more difficult to say no to her, but what the ties were or even if they existed I never learned.

Another overt nonformalized role that women fill concerns maintaining order at the fiestas. When asked the question of whose responsibility it is to maintain order at the fiestas, informants invariably reply that the mayordomo appoints two or three men who usually serve without pay, each taking a turn for an agreed upon period of time. This is correct, except that the information is incomplete. What has been elicited is a formalized public male role. Observation indicates that the formal policing action takes place outside the fiesta itself. These men guard the entrances to the fiesta and maintain order among the crowds of men that inevitably gather in the streets surrounding the place of the fiesta where portable cantinas are set up to sell beer. The complementary nonformalized role of maintaining order within the fiesta where the guests are all invited friends, compadres, and kinsmen of the hosts, is filled by women. My data, based on attendance at perhaps 25 fiestas of various kinds, suggests that whenever a male guest, encouraged by too much mezcal, begins to behave improperly, an elderly kinswoman intervenes. Commonly the man will leave his seat on the men's bench and begin to dance among the women. This is considered improper behavior since only women dance at fiestas except in two or three rigidly prescribed ritual contexts when certain men dance.[10] The woman, usually his aunt, grandmother, or on occasion, his madrina (fictive kin), first tries gentle persuasion to get the man to return to his seat. If this fails, she resorts to somewhat stronger statements about honor and shame. If the man continues to resist her efforts, something I witnessed only once, the woman will probably be joined by another woman or two, who help maneuver him near an exit, from which they forcibly push him into the street where the official "guards" take over.

Perhaps the most frequent context of women's overt nonformalized roles concerns sexual aggression. As has been pointed out in previous pages, the household's honor depends on the honor of its women. Any threat to the women's honor, therefore, demands action by the male household head against the transgressor. But the primary responsibility of avoiding and averting sexual overtures is placed on the women themselves. Women cooperate in overt nonformalized roles to protect one another from sexual aggression. Within the community what might be interpreted as improper advances on the part of a man are invariably associated with drinking. Therefore, women avoid any possibility of interaction with a drunken man by signaling one another of the approach of a borracho on the public streets, by ducking into one another's doorways and tienditas, and by many other avoidance techniques. It seems to be an unwritten law among Isthmus Zapotec women that women stand united in the face of the threat of any kind of unwanted or improper attention from a man, whether the man is stranger or brother. Such cooperative roles

---

[10]At fiestas certain important men and women dance the Zandunga. Both sexes dance at the same time and sometimes in pairs but without bodily contact. The Zandunga is a ritual dance performed at certain points during the fiestas.

\go beyond kinswomen and even beyond friends and neighbors. Any group of Zapotec women, whether in the market place, in the streets, or at a fiesta, whether known to one another or complete strangers, seems to close ranks spontaneously whenever there appears to be the slightest possibility of a threat to someone's "honor." When I was still a stranger in San Juan and did not know the rules of behavior, I several times found myself beckoned into the solar of a woman I had never seen before because a weaving, stumbling figure was approaching, often still half a block away.[11] A male informant claimed that women also cooperate in arranging and concealing one another's trysts with lovers. This certainly fits the pattern but it seems either to have been rare or absent among the women I knew best, none of whom ever referred to such cooperation.

Probably the most notable aspect of Isthmus Zapotec culture compared to our own is the degree of women's solidarity and esprit de corps. All women are assumed to have a common bond, that of protecting male kin from potentially violent confrontations with other men, of protecting themselves and their "sisters" from unwanted male attention, of protecting their own reputations as honorable women, and of caring for and protecting their children and other close kin from harm. Women can carry out these important duties only by banding together.

If a husband or son is drinking heavily in one of the many cantinas, women kin keep close tabs on what is happening. They may ask the tavern owner to notify them if trouble seems imminent or they may send a youngster to peek in on the situation now and then. If trouble threatens or if the man is becoming loud and uncontrollable his women relatives lose no time in going to the cantina to escort him home. It is my observation that men usually cooperate with their female rescuers and leave the scene without protest. This rescue operation by women relatives allows the men to extricate themselves from a dangerous situation without losing face.

If one's husband is drunk and potentially violent, the wife's mother, aunts, and sisters, and, yes, even mother-in-law and sisters-in-law, will arrange a "protection crew" who take turns staying with the threatened woman until the crisis has passed. A woman who does not take steps to protect herself and her children from male violence loses the respect of not just the women but the whole community.

Nonformalized cooperative roles among women are not limited to protection. Women cooperate in watching one another's puestos in the market place, in helping a neighbor carry her freight to the bus, in reporting undesirable actions of one another's teenage daughters, in reciprocal child care, and in other ways. Such cooperation often runs along kin lines but also includes neighbor's at home or in the market, comadres, and sometimes just acquaintances. In one instance, the male household heads of adjoining solares had not been on speaking terms for several years, yet the wives continued reciprocal economic transactions on a friendly basis

[11]During one phase of fieldwork I traveled with Jonsa and Elena, cousins who regularly sold Isthmus products in a market place some 350 miles distant. We spent from 10 to 14 days in the distant market place each time. On one occasion they concealed me for two days from an overly persistent suitor by stationing a ten-year-old sentry at the market entrance. Whenever the man approached, the signal was passed and I beat a hasty retreat out the rear entrance or hid in another woman's puesto. On another occasion Jonsa and Elena hid me from further verbal assaults by a drunken male market vendor (relative to one of the women vendors) after he began to use abusive language over U.S. involvement in Vietnam. In his case, the signal was passed whenever he left his puesto, headed our way, at which time I would duck into the neighboring woman's puesto where I could be neatly hidden from view by her pottery.

almost daily. As noted previously, women elders are the keepers of peace and order in the fiestas. They also have great authority within the extended kin network as arbiters of kin disputes and as enforcers of kin obligations.

Over the 20-year period since first fieldwork I have witnessed and had related to me many incidents in which women intervene to avert trouble between men and to protect one another from men's violence. I cannot relate them all here, but one particularly stands out as an example of the power of elder female kin. In 1982 a middle-aged male informant, reminiscing, recounted the following revealing incident from his childhood when his father, an alcoholic, was abusing the family.

> *Case 4:* Informant's mother (whom I had known during the last years of her life) had reached the limit of her endurance but, with five minor children and living patrilocally, saw no possibility of leaving. As a last recourse she sent for the husband's elderly aunt, his oldest female relative. The aunt, an unsteady wraith of an old woman dressed in the eternal black of widowhood, hobbled into the solar with the help of a cane and in her creaky voice (which informant imitated) immediately began to berate her nephew, a man in his early 50's, for his failings as a father and husband. While she scolded, she proceeded to beat him furiously across the shoulders with her cane.

My informant, also a man in his 50s when he related the incident, still recalled his childhood amazement that his father had not lifted a finger to protect himself. From the anthropological data presented in this case study, it was precisely the response to be expected. No Zapotec man, even the most inebriated, would be so disrespectful as to raise hand or voice to an elderly female relative. Nor in Zapotec culture is one ever too old to accept a child–parent reprimand from elder kin. The aunt, in spite of her frailty, undoubtedly felt a strong obligation to carry out her culturally prescribed duty to her nephew and his family.

Women's Covert Nonformalized Roles

Sometimes it is difficult or impossible to distinguish women's covert nonformalized roles from overt ones. In Case 5, which follows, what began as covert behavior on the part of the women actually became overt in regard to Abel when he learned of the incident before it was concluded and decided to "play along." Abel acknowledged the women's roles and gave his tacit approval by leaving the solar when he inadvertently learned of the trouble. He remained away until plenty of time had elapsed for the women to complete their plans. Often covert roles of Zapotec women seem to have the tacit approval of the menfolk they seek to manipulate. If not, they are viewed as being in the man's best interests and would have either his approval or that of his peers if known.

> *Case 5:* Abel, a bachelor in his mid-30s, lived in the solar where he was born with his elderly widowed mother, Doña Maria. The house was recognized by the entire family, including married siblings living elsewhere, as belonging to Abel. He had built it bit by bit over the years with his earnings as a bank teller. Abel was the fourth of five living siblings and the only surviving son of Doña Maria. All the sisters were married and living patrilocally. Since Doña Maria's health had begun to fail, and since she had no daughter-in-law to care for her, one of Abel's married sisters frequently came to clean up the solar and wait on Doña Maria, sometimes staying several days.

Abel had been planning for some time to install glass windows in the two back rooms of the house to improve air circulation in the solar. Doña Maria opposed his plan. Windows with glass panes are rare in San Juan mainly because of the open invitation they present to rock throwers and little boys with slingshots. In this case, however, the windows would open onto a big corral back of the house where Abel kept his oxen and horse. The footpath behind the corral was 60 yards or more from the house and the corral itself was enclosed with a rail fence. Abel thought it would be almost impossible for anyone to hurl a missile through the windows while passing on the footpath. He proceeded with his plan. About two weeks after the windows were installed, Abel's brother-in-law, Justino, arrived unannounced at the solar in a grossly inebriated state while Angela, Abel's sister and Justino's wife, was serving dinner to her ailing mother. An argument between the married couple ensued which ended by Abel throwing his brother-in-law into the street and telling him never to set foot inside the solar again. Abel, pale with rage, then left the solar and did not return until dawn. Angela spent the night in the solar with her mother. Sometime during the night Justino climbed into the corral at the rear of the house and heaved rocks through most of the forty or so panes in the new windows. Fortunately, the women were able to keep Abel from learning of the incident when he returned home briefly before going to work the following morning. When I talked to them later the same morning, they were terrified at the prospect of Abel finding out before the damage had been repaired. Both Doña Maria and Angela feared that a tragedy was imminent, one apt to prove fatal to one or both men. In order to do everything they could to avert tragedy, the women went into action.

Word was sent via a neighbor girl (also kin to family) to Abel's two sisters who resided in the pueblo. Both of them arrived shortly thereafter. The plan was to keep Abel and Justino apart at all costs. Margarita, Abel's elder sister, acting on behalf of her ailing mother, filed a formal complaint with the presidente which resulted in Justino's arrest and incarceration. With Justino safely behind bars and thus protected for the time being from Abel's justifiable rage an almost audible collective sigh of relief settled over the solar.

The next step was to have the windows repaired as quickly as possible. The women felt it was imperative that the windows be repaired by nightfall when Abel was expected to return. Doña Maria thought Abel's rage at this assault to his honor and position as household head would be less if no visual reminders of the episode remained when it finally came to his attention. A condition of Justino's release from jail was that he pay for the damages in full, a rather dim possibility considering his financial insolvency. Nonetheless, Donã Maria sent for a repairman to give an estimate of the costs of repairs. Abel's second sister, Jovita, then went to the solar of one of Justino's several sisters with the information. About two hours later Justino's youngest sister, an unmarried girl in her early twenties, arrived with $150 which she gave to Doña M., promising to return later with the remaining $50.

Abel returned home unexpectedly at noon and thus learned of the whole affair (he had probably already heard of it before he returned). Outwardly, he remained calm, and without uttering a word he turned on his heel and left the solar. He remained away for two days. By that time the windows were repaired, Justino was out of jail and, to my knowledge, the affair was never mentioned again by anyone concerned.

Justino's bold attack on Abel's property after the initial altercation was an open challenge to Abel's honor, to his position as head of the household, and to his formalized role of protector of his mother and sisters. It demanded retribution. Abel, although enraged, obviously wished to avoid bloodshed if possible. The cooperation of the women kinfolk of each of the two men made it possible for both to save face while avoiding the volatile face-to-face encounter the mores of the culture demanded.[12] It might be argued that the women of Abel's household acted on his behalf because he had no male kin to act for him, but the argument would not be valid in the case of Justino, whose father and brother both lived in San Juan. Although Justino and his brother maintained close personal ties, often cooperatively working their fields and exchanging labor and tools, it was not the brother but the three sisters who raised and delivered the $200 to Doña Maria.

Cases 6 and 7 both occurred prior to my fieldwork and were recounted to me in casual conversations. Possibly having interesting implications about the importance of nonformalized covert roles to the women themselves is the fact that Case 5 was actually told to me at least three different times by different women of the kin group. The incident, not particularly dramatic, had occurred more than two years earlier.

Case 6: When Abel's youngest sister married, it was his duty as head of the household to fill the role of the bride's deceased father. Being the brother of four sisters, Abel had always taken his role as protector of his sisters very seriously, particularly the youngest sister, Felipa, who was eight years his junior. Their mother apparently perceived that Abel might have difficulty making the sudden role switch, especially since the wedding was the aftermath of Felipa's elopement, which could have been interpreted as an insult to Abel's honor or as a failure on his part to control the improper behavior of his sister. Abel was a rather serious young man who ordinarily did not drink or frequent cantinas. None of the family had ever seen him inebriated. Even the small wedding fiesta that was planned would demand that Abel drink a rather large quantity of mezcal in the form of ritual toasts during the course of a few hours. Their mother feared he might become hostile and even violent under such conditions. To avoid potential trouble, a plan was devised. During the fiesta the womenfolk would keep Abel under close surveillance. At the first sign of threatening behavior on Abel's part, Doña Maria, physically too fragile to become involved herself, was to give the signal to Margarita, the eldest sister several years Abel's senior, and to Faustina, a distant cousin of Margarita's age who possessed the added advantage of sturdy build.

Margarita and Faustina were to flank Abel inconspicuously, laughing and joking, and sort of playfully dance him into a small adjoining room, get him into the hammock, leave, and lock the door. The plan was carried out successfully. Abel still wonders, according to the women, how he came to be in the room where he awoke the next morning.

The last example of women's covert nonformalized roles is interesting because it was recounted by an elderly woman informant in the course of reconstructing her life history spontaneously at my request. The incident had occurred about 35 years earlier and it is possible that Doña Isabel did not remember details precisely. She obviously recalled the events as a traumatic crisis in the course of her early married life.

Case 7: Around 1932 Doña Isabel was a young mother of two small daughters, living in a little lean-to in the rear section of her mother-in-law's solar. Her husband by common-

---

[12]Actually this is a general Latin American culture attitude and not peculiar to Isthmus Zapotec culture.

law marriage seems to have been 10 or 12 years her senior. Doña Isabel was about 25 years old. Her eldest child was about two and the other an infant. One day her husband announced he had found another woman, a *cantinera* in San Jacinto, with whom he was going to live. This placed Doña Isabel in a vulnerable position economically because her own father had strongly opposed her decision to live with her husband without benefit of a wedding ceremony. Now she could not turn to him or her brothers for help as would normally have been the case. She had no resources of her own and two infants to care for and support. Had she married in the Church she would have been able to count on her kinsmen and the couple's padrinos as well as her in-laws to bring pressure to bear on her errant husband to comply with his obligations. Doña Isabel did not accept her husband's decision passively, although he apparently began living with the other woman and was absent from his mother's solar for days on end. She had a strong ally in her widowed mother-in-law, however, who was incensed by her son's behavior. Whenever the husband, Celso, did come home, his mother would hide Doña Isabel and the children in the rear of her own house and tell her son they had moved out permanently and she did not know where they were. The two women carried on the ruse successfully for some time. Finally, Doña Isabel met him at the door on one of his visits, announced she had just returned, and stated she was willing to stay but only if he discontinued his relationship with the cantinera. Doña Isabel recounts that he agreed because he did not want to lose his children.

Isabel and Celso remained together for the rest of Celso's life and produced seven more children. When I asked if the reconciliation marked the end of her marital troubles, she replied, "Oh, no! We had disagreements many times but Celso's mother always took my part as long as she lived."

SUMMARY

In this chapter, I have tried to accomplish two objectives: 1) to explain how the concept of matrifocality aids in understanding Isthmus Zapotec women's roles and status and the reasons why Isthmus Zapotecs should properly be termed a matrifocal culture; and 2) to demonstrate through case material how women's nonformalized roles function to maintain the integrity of the household, to avoid conflict and violence, and more generally to lubricate the social machinery in a system where there exists a high level of fear and anxiety.

Both sexes recognize the importance of women's behavior in these nonformalized roles. At the same time the people themselves are sometimes unaware of the patterning and frequency of such behavior, which marks it as role behavior rather than random idiosyncratic situational behavior. The importance of women's nonformalized roles to the viability of the social system deserves emphasis. A man without womenfolk to "run interference" through the hazardous maze of social relations would be at a great disadvantage compared to the man with several kinswomen, those married into other households as well as those in his own solar. One wonders if José Luis of Case 2 would have been the innocent victim of an assassin's bullet had he not been warned of impending trouble by his sister. While women's nonformalized roles operate mainly through kinship (one of the informal structures recognized by Wolf), in the Isthmus Zapotec system it is the fact of gender rather than kinship which makes such roles possible, the fact that women operate in a social universe separate from men and, therefore, are privy to information that men either do not or may not circulate among themselves, and the fact that certain types of movements and courses of action are open only to women.[13]

Although the history of the development of matrifocality among the Isthmus Zapotecs is lost in the shadows of centuries past, the following scenario describes what might have occurred on the basis of what is known about Zapotec contemporary culture and recorded historical events. How well this reconstruction represents actual development can never be proven, yet I believe it has value in increasing our understanding of Isthmus Zapotec matrifocality as it exists today and of some of the underlying conditions that seem to foster matrifocality.

First, a comparison of matrifocality in other cultures offers convincing evidence that strong economic roles for women are probably a prerequisite. Economically, Isthmus Zapotec women have been active in the local markets for centuries. While it is not known when marketing became exclusively women's work, it is probable that the pressure to produce more after Contact to pay increasing tribute/taxes led to men spending more time in the fields and fishing, leaving women with more of the burden of selling the products men produced as time passed. A decreasing population in the first centuries of Spanish domination could only have exacerbated production pressures and placed the burden of paying tribute on fewer and fewer people.

Second, marketing, by putting cash in the hands of the women, led women to become the money managers at the household level. Few if any Zapotec campesinos even today hold the family purse strings. Instead, they ask their wives for spending money as they need it, and wives purchase most of the men's necessities: clothing, machetes, hats, huaraches, and carrying bags.

Third, women became the spokespersons and cultural brokers between their culture and the ruling culture. As women spent more time in the markets they acquired enough Spanish to function in their businesses in the Spanish-dominated market centers, while the men, working in the fields far away from the urban centers, had fewer opportunities to acquire the new language. Zapotec remained the first language, as it does today, but women's bilingual advantage over the menfolk resulted in women becoming the spokespersons for their households when dealing with outsiders.[14] Through bilingualism women became the translators and cultural interpreters between Spanish-mestizo and Zapotec cultures, a role they still often occupy.

A fourth factor in the blossoming of matrifocality was the matter of women's honor. The old Mediterranean notion that the family's honor depended on the honor of its women became firmly entrenched in Christian Mesoamerica. Most cultures could protect women's honor by restricting women's movements and interactions with outsiders. Not so for the Isthmus Zapotecs. Women's increasing importance as

---

[13]Women's ideologic place in Latin American culture generally is relevant to an understanding of Isthmus Zapotec women's roles also. For an excellent description, see Evelyn Stevens' "Marianismo: The Other Face of Machismo in Latin America."

[14]At the end of the 19th century, Frederick Starr reported of Isthmus Zapotec women: "They appear to decide most matters of importance and are the usual 'spokesmen' of the family . . . The traveler meets a constant line of ox-carts, each usually carrying a whole family. Should he ask his way . . . it is generally the woman . . . who responds" (Starr, 1900, p. 50).

marketers meant that they had to be free to move through the streets and markets, even in the Spanish-dominated centers. So girls were socialized to protect their own honor by observing a strict code of decorum when dealing with non-kin opposite sex and especially with non-Zapotec men. Such behavior is marked by belligerence and insult in the face of unwanted attention. Girls learn this behavior early because women depend on unmarried daughters to help with the marketing.

A fifth factor in the hypothetical evolution of matrifocality was women's solidarity. Women's solidarity manifested itself through the old but now defunct system of chaperonage, hostility toward aggressive men, and cooperation in the protection of lineal kin. Men's solidarity, in San Juan at least, is notably weak today. Whether that is a situation of recent origin or of long standing is unknown. Perhaps the fact that men work in isolation in the fields or with one or two close male kin most of their lives accounts for the lack of male solidarity. For women, however, solidarity remains staunchly entrenched. The obligation of women to protect their honor and their kin through solidarity and their individual actions was fully internalized by both genders some time in the past, its primary purpose being survival as a culture and as individuals during centuries of oppression and political domination by outsiders.[15]

Zapotec men were probably substantially more at risk of harm, even losing their lives, in encounters with the non-Zapotec power structure than were the women, leaving women in the position of shielding their male kin, whenever possible, from potentially dangerous interactions with powerful oppressors. It was also in the interest of female kin to protect men from succumbing to their own weaknesses by trying to keep inebriated male kin from involvement in potentially volatile conflicts.[16] Men's economic support, while not absolutely essential for survival, was and is extremely important to a family's economic security. All women, whether wife, mother, or sister, understand all too well the tragedy of a fatherless family.

In summary, matrifocality, fully internalized by both genders, has served both as an adaptation to cultural and political domination by outsiders and as a cultural mechanism through which the people were able to mitigate the impact of that domination. Women's roles as protectors of lineal kin of both sexes, women's roles as significant economic contributors to the household, and women's roles as stable, caring, trustworthy mothers and sisters can scarcely be overemphasized for the important part they have played in maintaining Isthmus Zapotec culture, ever-changing but still intact, during more than four centuries of domination and oppression by non-Zapotecs.

[15]Starr, an early ethnographer, was in the Isthmus in 1898 doing anthropometric research that required the precise physical measurement of various dimensions of the head, face, nose, limbs, among others. He was able to persuade San Juan men to cooperate and allow themselves to be measured but could not get any of the women to submit to be measured. In an eye-opening account of how Zapotecs were treated back then, he relates that in desperation he requested help from the El Centro police. Probably the mestizo police were only too eager to oblige. They captured San Juan women off the streets of El Centro and forcibly delivered their captives to Starr's office for measurement. Starr is silent about the women's reactions but one can imagine that San Juan women would not have submitted without a fight.

[16]Prior to the 16th century, only fermented and mildly intoxicating beverages were known in the New World. In Latin America, the Spaniards introduced the art of distilling and made potent alcohol available in the Americas for the first time.

9 / In-Betweens: A Third Gender[1]

ISTHMUS ZAPOTEC ATTITUDES TOWARD SEX AND GENDER ANOMALIES

Isthmus Zapotecs hold two contrasting attitudes concerning sex and gender. On the one hand, there are the cultural ideals of virginal brides, of women's honor, and other early Catholic teachings about sex and gender that seem to us prudish and victorian but which are still very much a part of the ideal culture the people carry in their minds and which Zapotec families still strive to maintain. On the other hand, there is an openness and acceptance of gender/sex "deviations" which we in America have traditionally lacked.

Muxe

A highly visible characteristic of Isthmus Zapotec populations is the *muxe*, or man–woman, a person who appears to be predominantly male but displays certain feminine characteristics. Many of these individuals seem to be what we in the United States would call transvestites, or cross–dressers.[2] Some are what we now call "gay," or persons who relate affectionately and erotically to persons of the same sex. In Zapotec culture the muxe fills a third–gender role between men and women, taking some of the characteristics of each of the other genders.

Although they are perceived as different from the general heterosexual male population, I found that muxe are neither devalued nor discriminated against in their community,[3] notable in that Isthmus Zapotecs, like all citizens of Mexico, have been dominated by European-derived Catholic ideology for over four centuries. Gender and sex-preference variations are something people deal with daily, and often in their own immediate families. Mestizos in El Centro may harass and even persecute muxe boys on occasion, but Zapotec parents (especially mothers and other women) are quick to defend them and their rights to "be themselves" because,

[1]An earlier version of Chapter 9 entitled "Isthmus Zapotec Berdaches" appeared in the Newsletter of the Anthropology Research Group on Homosexuality in 1985.

[2]A determination of the differences between heterosexual transvestites and homosexual transvestites would require sophisticated psychological and physical tests which have not been undertaken.

[3]Campbell (1990), who worked in a much larger community and focused on political actions, disputes my conclusions about the lack of discrimination. Our conflicting data come from different segments of the population and were collected in different social contexts. I spoke mainly with women and with men within family settings. Campbell, focusing on political events, not surprisingly collected much of his data in all male groups in political meetings and cantinas, the places where most political discussions among males take place. Once again it becomes apparent that the gender of the fieldworker and the gender of the informants and the physical settings of data gathering influence results.

as they put it, "God made them that way." I have never heard anyone suggest that a muxe boy has chosen his sexual orientation. To the people, the idea of choice of gender is as ludicrous as suggesting that one has a choice of skin color.

Little boys are tentatively identified as muxe by the family and community if they prefer playing house and dolls with little girls, if they imitate their mothers more than their fathers in play, or if they habitually enjoy dressing up in girl's clothing. Some boys, though, who display few of these characteristics in childhood still become muxe around the time of puberty. Others who acted "girlish" when small cast off this behavior in their teens and become indistinguishable from their non-muxe brothers, marry and raise families. A great deal more research needs to be carried out to understand the phenomenon of unpredictability of final outcomes.

Muxe are commonly believed to be the brightest, most gifted children of the family, a characteristic noted in other studies of non-Zapotec cross-gendered individuals.[4] Zapotec parents often consider them the best bet for educating beyond the level of other children in the family, but they will be kept in school beyond sixth grade only if they continue to show superior academic performance. This is understandable since most families cannot afford to educate all of their children even through sixth grade.

Some muxe do certain women's work such as embroidering women's fiesta costumes and sewing items of women's clothing, decorating house altars, and drawing designs for embroidery—all means of earning money. Others do traditional men's work such as making silver and gold jewelry. Besides being thought to be exceptionally intelligent, they have a reputation for having artistic abilities and the women's work they do is said to be done more artistically and with greater care than when women do it. Nowadays, muxe often find white-collar jobs in banks, government offices, and businesses—jobs that traditionally have been viewed as men's work in Mexican culture although today (1990) women also fill some of these white-collar positions. In the Isthmus, muxe men have recently become heavily involved in local politics, even to the point of election to the presidency of the municipio.[5]

On occasion young adult muxe wear cosmetics and such feminine items as high-heeled pumps, neither of which is traditionally used by Zapotec women. Their hair is cut male-style but usually combed in more feminine ways than is the usual male practice. Their mode of dress is predominantly male, consisting of men's trousers and shirts, but with more care taken as to fit, quality of fabric, and tailoring than is the case with most heterosexual males. Sometimes muxe wear gold earrings or necklaces and have gold-coin buttons made for their shirts. In private they sometimes wear mestizo-style women's dresses.

In contrast to traditional "berdaches" in many North American Indian cultures, muxe have no special religious role although it is possible that they did in former times. On the other hand, they are in no way excluded from religious rites in the community. In the folk Catholicism practiced today, adult married muxe participate as other men. They are not barred from sponsoring public fiestas, a major avenue to

[4]See, for example, Money and Ehrhardt (1972).
[5]See also Campbell (1990).

prestige, nor are they prohibited from participating fully in any of the other rites appropriate for men. However, young muxe are permitted certain public behavior at the fiestas not appropriate for other men, such as couple-dancing with women and with each other. As previously noted, heterosexual men do not dance in couples with either sex but perform only traditional dances such as the *Zandunga*, a dance in which men and women circle around each other without touching. Women, though, are expected to dance together in close body contact, just as it is natural and expected that women show much public affection toward one another.[6] At fiestas it is considered very unseemly for a woman *not* to dance with her sisters, female first cousins, mother, and comadres. Isthmus Zapotec culture allows both women and men more freedom in expressing affection for same-sex friends in public than is the case in American culture. Among women, there are no sexual innuendos in such behavior that I could ever detect. Elderly men walk down the street hand-in-hand, as do women of all ages and relationships. Women also stand with arms entwined in public, a gesture expressing friendship and sisterly affection.

Young muxe may dance with women, most often their mothers, sisters, or cousins, just as though they were women; and they also dance with other muxe. In the context of fiesta dancing then, muxe may take the role of women although not the costume. However, the same individual does not take the men's ritual role *and* dance in the woman's role on the same occasion, nor even in the same life phase. Many of the group referred to herein as muxe are *not* homosexual, there being no inevitable connection between transvestism and homosexuality. And, of course, as in many cultures, including our own, there are a number of homosexual males who are publicly invisible because their overt behavior is the same as other males. Hence, it is not surprising that some Zapotecs who are known as muxe marry and raise families. Those who are identified as muxe in Zapotec culture seem to be considered as a third gender, different from either men or women, yet combining characteristics of both.

Marimachas

As in a majority of, if not all, human populations, there are also a few Zapotec women who are masculine in behavior. Referred to by the Spanish word *marimacha*, they are not culturally recognized as essentially different from other women although physically they appear more masculine and sometimes display hostile, aggressive behavior. They neither dress differently from other women nor use different hair styles. What seems to identify them in the community is their physically more masculine appearance and behavior and their preference for masculine work even though only one marimacha known to me (in 1985) has taken a man's occupation fulltime—self-employed chauffering of a public conveyance for hire. Marimacha women are not nearly as visible as muxe men, and it is my

---

[6]Recently, one fieldworker published the erroneous and misleading statement, based on fleeting exposure to the culture, that all Isthmus Zapotec women are "more or less lesbians." I expect she will retract that irresponsible and wholly false statement after her current period of fieldwork is completed.

impression that they are considerably fewer in number in the pueblo than their male counterparts. Zapotec culture does not consider them nor do they consider themselves as a separate gender category.

Bisexuality

Bisexuality among both males and females may be more common than strict homosexuality. And Zapotecs are as tolerant of bisexuality as they are of transvestism and homosexuality. On the basis of my observations, bisexuals, or persons who have both heterosexual and homosexual predilections, almost always marry and raise families and often it is only late in life that the community becomes aware that the individual "has turned homosexual." Now and then a man or a woman leaves a heterosexual marriage after many years to establish a homosexual relationship in middle age, scarcely raising an eyebrow among the neighbors, although that is not to say thay they condone such behavior. One must be reminded that tolerating such behavior and condoning it are very different propositions. Over the 20-plus years I have worked in San Juan, several prominent citizens with grown children have left their heterosexual mates to live with same-sex partners. To my knowledge there are only whispers about the change of status for a short while but no real ostracism.

Persons who publicly become same-sex couples seemingly experience little change in their community life. They continue to attend fiestas as before, fulfilling the fiesta behavior expectations of their sex. This is particularly easy to do because there are virtually no heterosexual couple interactions in religious contexts. Genders are always seated in different places at religious festivals and have different roles and duties throughout. Heterosexual couples often do not even attend fiestas as a couple but as individual representatives of their households, one or the other attending as appropriate.

Younger, unmarried women may also become involved in lesbian relationships on occasion although this seems to be much rarer than the involvement of older, married women.[7,8] In the single case of which I have knowledge, the unmarried eldest daughter of a close friend and informant left her mother's home and took up residence in another barrio with her older lesbian lover. The daughter was then 25 years old, not yet beyond the expected age of heterosexual marriage, which might have been a factor in the mother's consternation. The daughter's action proved so upsetting to the mother that relations between the two broke off in bitterness. A reconciliation of sorts occurred a year later, and the daughter continues to live with her lesbian partner now nearly a decade later, visiting her natal family infrequently.

[7]Recent publications on native North American berdaches include Greenberg, Whitehead, and Williams, the latter the most ambitious attempt yet on this broad and complex subject.

[8]Recent publications on homosexuality cross-culturally include Williams, Herdt, as well as Adams and several others in Blackwood (1986a). Only a few anthropologists have researched or even mentioned lesbianism cross-culturally. Sources include Blackwood (1986b), Lockard (1986), and Whitehead (1981).

SUMMARY AND CONCLUSIONS

Research on gender and sexual variations is still far from a stage where definitive statements can be offered as to causes, but a few tentative suggestions seem appropriate. Although no attempt has been made to establish the incidence of sex/gender variability in San Juan, it appears higher in the Isthmus Zapotec populations than among other indigenous populations of Mexico. Rymph collected some data incidentally in one small Isthmus Zapotec community in the early 1970s and found a frequency rate of six percent male transvestism (muxe). In contrast, a study of Valley Zapotec deviance by Selby (1974) concludes unequivocally that homosexuality does not exist there. He does not even mention transvestism, leaving one to assume that this phenomenon is absent as well.

There is evidence that male transvestism and homosexuality "run in families." In one Isthmus family of my acquaintance, five of six sons are muxe, while a sixth, a middle-aged father of seven children, exhibits mild effeminate behavior. Zapotecs themselves believe that these sex/gender anomalies have a genetic base. Scientific evidence too seems to be building for a genetic or *in utero* developmental basis. Zapotec communities consisting of relatively small interbreeding populations and the apparently relatively high gender variation in the region would fit the expected pattern of a genetic component. A 1986 Boston University study by Pillard and Weinrich lends support to the involvement of inherent factors.[9]

But of more interest to the cultural anthropologist is the enlightened and tolerant attitude of the population toward sex and gender variations. From their simple lifestyle and low level of formal education, some might consider the Isthmus Zapotecs an unsophisticated people, yet we could all learn from their open-minded and accepting attitudes in respect to sex/gender variations.

[9]The study compared a sample of 101 American males ages 25–35, of whom 50 were gay, for sexual variability of other family members. Twenty percent (20%) of gay men had brothers who were predominantly or exclusively homosexual compared to only four percent (4%) of the heterosexual males.

10 / Conclusion

IMAGES, PUBLIC AND PRIVATE

In summing up women's roles and the concept of matrifocality, it will be helpful to keep in mind the distinction between real and ideal culture. In the field, the anthropologist usually finds there are disparities between what people say they do and what she observes that they do. Real culture is what people actually do while ideal culture is the mental image they hold of what is proper, what they have been taught they should do. Primary school books in the United States have presented the nuclear family as two parents, two children and the dog, mother as homemaker, father as income-producer, living in a white cottage on a quiet small-town street, the ideal culture. Yet most children's real families have not fit this ideal mold for decades, if indeed they ever did so. Zapotec culture's ideal is the patriarchal family, with patrilocal residence, virginal brides, and morally superior mothers who nurture the family and guard its honor. Only some of these ideals are met by some people part of the time, yet the patterns of the cultural ideal remain firmly fixed in the minds of the people just as the nuclear family in the white cottage remains firmly fixed in our ideas of what should be. In both cases, actual day-to-day life reveals the real pattern. In San Juan the close observation of and participation in women's daily lives reveal the central place of women in economic, political, religious, and social-control contexts, i.e., matrifocality.

A popular stereotype in Mexican national culture views Isthmus Zapotec women as assertive, dominant individuals who favor strong language and ribald behavior, presumably in contrast to other Mexican women. This stereotype, which does not fit Mexican cultural ideals, is based in part on observations of real behavior in the context of public fiestas and markets and in part on the nature of the Zapotec language, which is graphic and explicit. Body parts and bodily functions are not taboo words in Zapotec.[1] Indeed, it has been claimed that there are no taboo words at all in Zapotec. Such words only become obscene in translation into languages which consider them obscene, leading to ethnocentric gross misinterpretations of the women (and men and children) who use words outsiders consider taboo in everyday speech. To view Zapotecs, and especially women, in such simplistic and ethnocentric stereotypes is as ludicrous as stereotyping all Louisianans according to their ribald public behavior during Mardi Gras.

As the reader has learned in Chapter 8, women are taught to repel unwanted

---

[1]As an example of Zapotec language usage, a young mother in the home where I have lived on several occasions often called her baby daughter the Zapotec equivalent of "little vagina" as a term of endearment.

attention from men, especially those of the socially and economically dominant mestizo culture. As described in previous pages, conditions of life of Isthmus Zapotec women make it necessary to move about in public while a traditional Latin American cultural ideal is that a "lady" rarely appears in public places, especially alone. In a social system in which family honor hinges on women's virtue and in which women must be free to pursue their selling-buying ventures in many public places, it becomes imperative that women behave in ways designed to leave no doubt in anyone's mind as to their intentions. For this reason, Isthmus Zapotec girls are socialized early to rebuff undesirable attention.[2]

Members of both sexes greatly admire a "woman who defends herself" by devastatingly insulting remarks directed toward would-be lotharios. Whenever I complained to women informants of unpleasantly familiar encounters with men in El Centro, in Oaxaca, or elsewhere, I was told that it was my own fault because I did not "defend" myself. I did eventually learn the technique of defending myself by insult and found it effective enough although, true to my gringa enculturation, I could never rid myself of uncomfortable guilt at being so "rude and impolite" according to the teachings of my own culture.

Perhaps I have over-emphasized the don't-fool-around-with-me attitude that is so ingrained in women's personalities that I have neglected the opposite side of their personalities. Isthmus Zapotec women can also be fun-loving and coquettish and some, often older women after drinking beer for hours at fiestas, tease men with suggestive language. People take this for what it is, a little fun and relaxation in an otherwise hard and somber existence. This has led some observers to the conclusion that "Isthmus women will do anything." Nothing could be further from the truth.

In the more intimate contexts of neighborhood and solar, women's behavior is quite different from their stereotyped public image constructed in part from real behavior and in part through the misinterpretations of travelers and mestizos writers. On the intragroup level of social relations, I found women modest, decorous, considerate of others, gentle, empathetic, and indulgent of children and elders. These same characteristics also mark the behavior of Zapotec men under normal circumstances and in similar contexts. Thus, the significant dichotomy between intragroup and intergroup behavior must be borne in mind in descriptions of the behavior of the people of San Juan Evangelista. Whereas in intragroup relationships there are strong sanctions against conflict and violence (although they occur with frequency), such sanctions are relaxed when intergroup relationships are involved, especially when actions of the outgroup are perceived as threats to members of the community.

In San Juan adults of either sex will come to the aid of any member of the community who seems to be threatened by outsiders (which includes district, state, or federal police). As history and current events amply demonstrate, women are

[2]In 1972 while a field ethnology class I was heading was visiting the Isthmus, a parked taxicab driver, noting that we were all gringas, was emboldened to indelicately prod a student sitting on a stool at a sidewalk beverage stand. Of course, there was a shriek from the student, at which my Zapotec comadre, in a voice which could be heard across the central plaza and into the market (the intent was obviously a public announcement) let out a string of insults in mixed Spanish and Zapotec. Pointing out the deficiencies in the character of the taxicab driver that would lead him to such an uncouth act, the language, if translated into any of the European languages, would have made Popeye the Sailor blush.

often and regularly active in repelling threats to the homefront and have the advantage of "getting by with" acting aggressively toward the dominant power structure with less fear of reprisal than the men. Time and again throughout history, and continuing today, women do not hesitate to use abusive language, rocks, and *palos* (clubs) against armed contingents whom they perceive as threats. Some have lost their lives in such encounters and others have been injured and jailed.

It may seem paradoxical that in a culture where roles are clearly delineated by sex, the people are not overly concerned with deviations from such roles nor with sex as a status marker. In San Juan, one is first a human being, an individual, and only second and incidentally a man or woman. While the sexes are usually segregated, perform different tasks, wear distinct clothing, and behave differently, none of these differences is viewed as marking the essential inferiority of one sex in relation to the other. Women who choose to or must take on male tasks on occasion are not criticized as unfeminine nor are men who do women's tasks by necessity or choice.

The phenomenon of *machismo,* so often cited by North Americans as a male characteristic in Latin American cultures, seems to be largely absent in intragroup relations in Zapotec culture. Where such behavior is evident, it is negatively sanctioned. A man who acts "muy macho" is derided as an overbearing bully, and a woman who mistreats or takes advantage of one weaker than she is similarly criticized (for example, a mother who strikes her child).

Comparing Isthmus Zapotec women to middle-class women in the United States, I discovered some surprising differences. I have already noted the *esprit de corps* among Zapotec women, probably their most notable distinction compared to North America, where women's solidarity, until the recent Women's Movement, has been so distressingly lacking. This posture of female solidarity, which goes beyond kinship and beyond ethnicity, allows Zapotec women to cooperate in many situations where it would be impossible for men to do so. But apart from this, Zapotec women seem to possess a self-identity as part of a universal sisterhood. They assume, naively to be sure, that their goals, aspirations, and desires are shared by all womankind. They do not view themselves as competing with other women for men's favors, they do not seek their own self-identity through men, nor do they view themselves as dependent on men to any greater extent than men are dependent on women. In San Juan survival requires the effort of every able person in the household and no member's contribution is considered insignificant.

Zapotec women are affectionate toward one another and sometimes express jealousy of a friend's or comadre's friendships with other women, often in a lighthearted, half-joking manner. I found no lesbian overtones in affection and mild jealousy expressed between women. Possibly mild jealousy is an expression of the high value placed on friendship, an avidly sought relationship for the entire culture, but one that appears to be difficult to maintain. That could be a compelling reason for the great viability of compadrazgo, which cements friendship relations into more binding and formal fictive kin ties.

Another admirable quality of Isthmus Zapotec women is their ability to refrain from open criticism and disdain toward other women, in fact toward anyone. I spent untold hours listening to and taking part in casual conversations among women, sometimes in large groups gathered to prepared food for a fiesta, sometimes in groups of market vendors and their customers, more often in small groups of kinswomen and neighbors, and frequent and extended conversations stretching over many months with two unrelated extended families whose members acted as key informants. The occasions on which women expressed criticism, disdain, or derision toward another person were so rare that they still stand out in my memory.

CHANGES, 1967–1990

With modern transportation and modern communication the world in the last half of the 20th century has become immeasurably smaller. In microcosm the same things that minimize the world enlarge formerly isolated people's world view. For the Isthmus Zapotecs, their world is widening through more cultural contacts with the industrialized world.

Peasant societies are usually considered culturally conservative and slow to change. By modern U.S. standards changes have come slowly to Zapotec campesinos, yet Zapotecs have always been a changing people, and they have demonstrated through centuries their great ability to adapt to changing conditions. Despite their fierce independence, Isthmus Zapotecs have not been politically autonomous for five, perhaps six or more centuries. Nonetheless, they have managed to survive as an ethnically distinct population. They readily adopted a vast number of sixteenth-century Spanish culture traits and they adapted their own culture to the demands of colonial rule. Changes wrought by Mexican Independence and the 1910 Revolution have been extensive. Colonial era technology (oxcarts, Mediterranean plows) and behavior patterns (folk Catholicism rites and customs) continue not because Isthmus Zapotecs reject other patterns out of hand but rather because their cultural system remains viable in their socioeconomic environment.

Women of San Juan Evangelista have accepted new ideas and adopted new ways as eagerly as have the men, sometimes with even more enthusiasm. Decades ago women saw the great advantages in treadle sewing machines and mechanical nixtamal mills. Today they buy blenders and propane cooking ranges because they recognize the convenience and utility of these appliances.

Women's costume, although always subtly changing, has remained basically traditional in spite of the schools' edicts which require mestizo-style uniforms. In the 1960s girls were allowed to wear traditional dress to schools in San Juan (but not in El Centro). In 1990 San Juan schools all required uniforms of both boys and girls on the pattern of national schools. As a result girls who attend school become accustomed to wearing knee-length tailored skirts and blouses which might lead to the adult woman wearing western-style clothing. It was encouraging to note in 1990 that teenage girls and young married women often revert to traditional dress at home. A teacher and friend–informant for 25 years who wore western-style dresses in her younger years in 1990 was again dressing in huipil and long skirts outside the classroom. Beauty, comfort, modesty, ease of movement, and ease of care are strong incentives to retain the traditional woman's costume while the rising cost of fabrics may be working against its continued use.

Since 1979 when the large oil-refining plant in the nearby port city of Salina Cruz began operation, the rate of change (with both positive and negative consequences) has accelerated notably. In the final pages of this volume, a number of these changes are discussed in more detail, with special emphasis on changes which have occurred since 1979.

Demography

The fundamental change in San Juan Evangelista as in the world as a whole is the growth of the population. While the region has experienced a great influx of non-Zapotecs attracted to the Salina Cruz oil-refining complex, San Juan's growth has been through natural increase and through the slowing of out-migration due to increased regional job and business opportunities.

Before the building of the refinery, begun in 1974 and inaugurated in 1979, Salina Cruz was a port town of about 25,000 people. Ten years later, 1989, it was reported to have 180,000 inhabitants, many of them immigrants from other parts of Mexico. The major Zapotec market center has grown from perhaps 35,000 in 1967 to 90,000 in 1989, while San Juan, around 8,000 in 1967, is now bursting out of its seams on all sides with a population of between 15,000 and 20,000. There is so little room into which to expand, because of hills, river, and adjacent city that Juanecos have established an unofficial colony across the river to absorb the overflow. Urban growth has been chaotic and frantic. Houses crowd up to the top of

A New Choza Home on the Riverbank (1990)

the hills and down across the river levee to the edge of the nearly dry river channel. Most of the houses are of concrete block, the modern building material of choice, which does not require plaster and paint for maintenance as did the old adobe buildings. With dirt-colored block buildings, streets now paved the same concrete gray, and the few majestic old trees removed to make way for more houses and more streets, the town has taken on a ghostly cast relieved only by the brightly painted walls of the older adobe buildings in the center of the town.

Population, Modernization, and the Environment

In 1967 the Mexican government's first large-scale attempt at economic development of the region, the Benito Juarez Dam and Reservoir (built to irrigate over 50,000 hectares of land) was only in the first stages of operation. The river had already been reduced to a seasonal sewer but still flushed itself periodically by the release of water from the dam during the rainy season. In 1990 after several years of dry weather and continued dumping of raw sewage and solid wastes into the river by upstream communities, the river, for centuries an important source of food and recreation for the people of San Juan, has become a permanent mosquito-breeding open sewer which threatens public health.

The refinery, while employing relatively few Juanecos often temporarily or at the lowest-paying jobs, has led to an increased demand for locally-grown food, particularly beef, pork, fruits, and maize. The larger market for their products has benefitted San Juan, a major "breadbasket" municipio of the region, by expanding its market.

The negative side of the refinery complex and the population increase has been the wholesale degradation of the environment. Oil spills have destroyed beaches and wildlife while air pollution from the refinery and increased vehicular traffic has sullied the once-crystal skies. Conditions will probably not improve in the foreseeable future. In December 1990 Pemex announced that the capacity of the oil refinery will be increased from its present production of 230 thousand barrels per day to 540 thousand barrels daily by 1992, making it the largest refinery in the Americas and one of the two largest in the world. (El Imparcial, December 2, 1990).

Aside from the environmental pollution, wildlife is being wiped out by a burgeoning population. The Pacific Coast iguanas may already be extinct. Those coming into the markets in 1990 are very small and often of sub-species not formerly seen. They are reported to come from the trans-Isthmus areas to the north of San Juan. Trade in sea turtle eggs, an endangered species, continues although forbidden by law. Armadillos, already getting rare in 1982, are now seldom seen in area markets. Experiments in iguana farming being carried out in Panama and Costa Rica have been found to produce more protein at vastly less expense per unit of land than the ubiquitous cattle. Such ranch-hatched semi-domesticated iguanas could be an important future source of food for Isthmenians and one which would preserve rather than destroy native scrub forests.

El Centro, long the hub of San Juan marketing, seems now to be evolving into a bedroom city for refinery employees. At the same time, San Juan appears to be becoming economically independent from El Centro to a much greater degree than formerly. El Centro's marketplace business appears to be shrinking while that of San Juan is growing. San Juan's market now operates all day every day. Where formerly San Juan women had to go to El Centro to sell their products and make most food purchases, neither is now necessary. In addition to the availability of an abundance of foods in the San Juan market, there is a block-long clothing and household goods market held in the street adjacent to the marketplace weekly. A post office and public telephones in San Juan further increase its independence from El Centro.

San Juan itself may have reached an environmental low point between 1982 and 1985 when it seemed that the amount of nonbiodegradable refuse collecting in the streets would soon overwhelm and bury its residents. Since then a sanitation program has been pursued, much to the credit of the several recent presidentes, their ayuntamientos, and the citizens of San Juan who appear to be working together in an unprecedented spirit of community to pave streets, collect garbage (still dumped in two unsightly mountains on the rural edge of town), connect houses to a central sewer system, and keep pigs confined to pens. Much of this laudable effort has been made in preparation for the successful bid for the status of *villa,* a promotion from the former official status of pueblo, a *fait accompli* in October 1990, and to a first-time-ever visit by a Mexican president earlier in the same year.[3]

San Juan's potable water problems, which began in 1974–1975 coincidental with construction of the refinery and continued until the late 1980s, have now been partially, though not permanently, solved by the construction of a municipal water storage facility of its own.

Health

A positive change since 1982 is an apparent decrease in small child mortality. With no reliable statistics available, I must base this judgment on the fact that there were no infant deaths during the month of fieldwork in 1990 while there were three in the first two weeks of fieldwork in 1982. The improved water supply must get a good share of the credit since most infant deaths in the past have been caused by impure water, according to local doctors.

Obesity in people over 35 (and sometimes much younger) is a problem affecting many people's health. Diabetes, damaged hearts, and cancer are the big three causes of deaths of people over 50, and a diet high in sugar and animal fat along with culturally encouraged obesity are high on the list of contributing factors. Government-sponsored diabetes clinics are held from time to time to teach about and encourage a more healthful diet, but only people who already know or suspect they suffer from the disease attend.

The greatest air and noise polluters in San Juan in 1990 are the motos, those three-wheel runabouts made from small motorcycles and scooters which replaced the local bus–taxi–porter system several years ago. There are now 100 motos in San Juan, with a ban placed on licensing more. Convenience and low fares have made them everyone's transportation of choice and severely cut into the taxi business

[3]To gain official status as villa a community must have at least 15,000 residents, paved streets, electricity, drainage system, post office, public telephone, market structure, and several other public amenities. The advantage to the community is that a villa qualifies for government benefits on more favorable terms than a pueblo.

whose unionized drivers are trying to get motos and their unionized drivers banned. Mercifully, a former source of noise pollution, the several public revolving loud speakers mounted on poles and turned to top volume to better catch every ear, have been muffled except for certain brief periods of the day.

Cosmetic improvements to the pueblo since 1982 include painting the churches (paid for by the xuanas), constructing walled gardens in the central plaza and around the ancient church, and paving streets in the upper half of the town. For the president's visit new lamps were installed along the main street, streetside flower-beds were created, and potted plants set to adorn otherwise barren spots. Old buildings, even abandoned ones, were repaired on the street side and freshly painted along the route walked by the presidential entourage.

At the domestic level, modernization has taken the form of cement-block construction of houses and walls, sewer connections, more flush toilets and show-ers, more propane cooking stoves. Television sets are in the majority of homes, even many with few other modernities. Sadly, the quality of television programs I have witnessed leads me to doubt whether television is teaching people anything useful or even offering them anything approaching a reflection of the real urban, modernized western world beyond their borders. Along with increasing quantities of junk food, people now have the dubious advantages of junk television. Refrigera-tors, formerly merely little-used status symbols, are in more homes and are actually being used to preserve food by a growing minority of women. Stereos are promi-nently displayed in some homes. Automobiles and trucks, the ultimate status symbols of a material nature, are owned by a relatively small but growing number of families. Sometimes several vehicles are to be found carefully parked inside the solar and covered with tarpaulins to keep off the dust.[4] Given the opportunity, young women as well as young men learn to drive.

Among the 20- to 35-year-old generation of Juanecos there are now a number of white-collar technicians, semi-professionals, and professionals who are able to get middle-level jobs in the area, at the refinery or in the local schools as teachers, making it less essential to migrate to the cities. These jobs have helped some lucky families in San Juan greatly because government health care is provided not only for the immediate nuclear family of the worker but also for his/her parents. Education continues to be stressed by the national government and is valued by most parents, but there continues to be minimal education for many children and none at all for an unfortunate minority. One of the developing problems of San Juan will be sharper socioeconomic division between educated, middle-class families and the under-educated campesino segment of the community.

Political Changes

Always a sore spot for PRI-dominated Mexico, during the past decade the Isthmus has made national headlines more than once because of the violence-

---

[4]Many household heads who own vehicles have not learned to drive but depend on an adult child to chauffer them. For most families, passenger cars are little used except when taking trips to Oaxaca, Mexico City, or other destination more than 100 miles distant, the reason being that private vehicles are more of a nuisance than a convenience for shorter trips where local public buses, motos, or taxicabs are available.

wracked protests and ultimately successful election of COCEI candidates to the ayuntamiento of Juchitan in 1984 and again in 1989. San Juan has its own COCEI group, but it has not as yet proved powerful enough to gain a majority vote in the local ayuntamiento. The major change in San Juan has been the election of a PRI ayuntamiento in 1989 that included the first-ever woman to fill one of the five regador offices.[5] She has taken as her special task the project of organizing women's cooperatives. Attempts to organize a food-buying cooperative for very poor woman-headed households was not successful in 1990, but prospects for a marketing cooperative of 400 totoperas appeared to have more chance of success. If successful, it will be the first women's cooperative in San Juan. However, the Regadora de Hacienda has a tough job ahead of her and faces tremendous opposition and pressure. Anonymous threats have been made on her life along with those of the other office-holders, and their prospects of peacefully fulfilling their terms, let alone accomplishing much of significance, seem depressingly slim.

Religion

The fiesta system has been gradually changing since well before 1967 to less emphasis on the sponsorship of public fiestas and more emphasis on the private life-crises fiestas as a means of raising family prestige. All over the region public fiestas to patron saints are becoming more commercialized, many now conducted as income-generating enterprises with a hefty admission charge, and the aggressive selling of beer, snacks, and souvenirs.

In San Juan, fiesta activity reflects economic cycles. In 1990 with everyone complaining of slow business and no money, noncritical life-crisis rites such as weddings and anniversary mixa gue´ tu´ were postponed or conducted on a smaller than usual scale.

Among younger, educated Juanecos the old beliefs in witchcraft, divining, and spirit possession are giving way to more secular and scientifically-based ideas; but among people under 40 with little education, as well as the over-40 inhabitants, the old beliefs seem as strong as ever. Beliefs about death and spirits of the dead are among the most steadfast of religious beliefs. In 1990 local spiritualists and amateurs were being contacted regularly by spirits of Juanecos' deceased relatives, wishing to speak to persons of their family. Spirits also often contact family members directly without going through a third party. A 40-year-old informant talks with her sister, deceased ten years, in the family home on a regular basis, while the niece of a long-deceased wealthy man repeatedly contacts his widow with the news that she (the niece) is the medium through which the husband wishes to speak to her. The widow, being of sound mind, is skeptical and questions why her husband's spirit does not come to his own home to speak with her directly rather than going through the niece.

Native curers are still important and respected. San Juan's most widely-known

[5]The Regadora de Hacienda is about 36 years old and holds the degree of Engineer in Metallurgical Chemistry. She worked in her profession in other parts of Mexico for several years but returned to live with her parents about 10 years ago. She is a single mother with two daughters and supported herself and children before her election to the ayuntamiento by teaching in local schools. She has no plans to return to the profession for which she was trained.

curer, Nino Cabeza, who died in 1955, was considered important enough to be given a prominent place in the local history prepared in 1990 to commemorate the town's elevation to villa.

Fundamental Protestantism (known as evangelismo in Mexico) is gaining converts all over Latin America including San Juan. Jehovah's Witnesses established a following among the potters beginning about 1966. Then the poorest and landless segment of the population, the potter families, still strong adherents to their adopted religion, have prospered by withdrawing from the alcohol-saturated fiesta rituals and learning new skills and health-maintenance techniques. They have even been able to purchase small plots of farmland and some potter families engage in several businesses as well. In 1990 there were some 300 members in this congregation. Although Jehovah's Witnesses have not gained many adherents outside the pottery-making community, the economic gains they have made have not gone unnoticed by the rest of the community.

Recently, a fundamental Baptist church has become very active in San Juan, attracting some of the better educated professionals and others. In late 1990 they had under construction a large concrete-block church on the reclaimed land of the river border. The "new" religions have obviously benefitted some individuals and families by extricating them from alcoholism and fiesta obligations and establishing healthier lifestyles. Whether they will have a beneficial influence on the community as a whole in the long run remains in doubt. As has already occurred in Central America, fundamental evangelism can increase divisiveness within communities and speed the disintegration of indigenous cultures and languages. If it becomes a force in San Juan, one would hope people could pull out the positive aspects, such as abstinence from alcohol, to apply to their lives, while rejecting those divisive and narrow attitudes which mark most of the fundamentalist sects as intolerant of diversity.

Social Aspects of San Juan, 1990

Without doubt, violence, alcoholism, and some seemingly still small drug trade are San Juan's greatest immediate challenges. Without a trained and equipped police force, it is difficult to the tenth power to maintain a community of over 15,000 people free of crime. Homicide is epidemic in the region, with at least seven or eight occurring each year in San Juan alone.[6] Targeted victims are inevitably male although innocent passersby are occasionally hit by stray bullets during the lamentably frequent public shoot-outs and assassinations.[7] During the 1990 fieldwork period the town was unusually peaceful, a condition residents attributed to the lingering after effects of the Mexican president's visit.

Alcoholism seems to be claiming victims at a younger age, cases of alcoholic

---

[6]My homicide statistics collected for the years 1974, 1975, and 1981 are seven, seven, and more than eight, respectively.

[7]In 1990 a longtime informant recounted that men with guns had come to the cantina across from her house a few months before, looking for an elderly neighbor with whom they had quarrelled. Shots were fired, one entering the front window of her house and exiting through the back patio. She, her daughter, and small grandchild were in the house at the time and crouched in a corner of an inside room until the violence had subsided. The elderly man was killed.

husbands and fathers in their 20s and 30s becoming more frequent. Campbell (1990) blames the beer distributors for increased alcoholism, but to my mind that blame must be shared by a fiesta system that forces men to drink prodigious quantities of mezcal within a few hours and leaves them unconscious. There is no doubt that alcohol and its misuse are the major reasons for family anguish and suffering, much of which falls on the wife who tries to deal with an abusive husband, eke out a living with little help from him, and keep the family together.[8]

Gender relations have not changed as far as the importance of women in keeping men from violent encounters or the importance of women's economic contribution to the households. What may change women's position relative to men in the future is the rise of wage and salaried work for men, which places them more directly in control of their earnings. Historically over the world men's steady paid labor, whether unskilled or professional, has too often resulted in unilateral dependence of women on men and the consequent loss of status for women. A second factor which may alter gender relations in San Juan is the trend toward more educated men marrying traditional, unschooled women. This has become more common since the refinery began operation, making it possible for men with education to find local employment instead of migrating to Mexico City, where they often marry non-Zapotec women. Young women who acquire professional educations, of course, also often marry non-Zapotecs and there are fewer opportunities for professionally trained women locally. Although I perceive that up to now gender relations have remained much as I first described them in the traditional families, the changes of modernization do not bode well for women's continued equality along traditional parameters.

An encouraging sign of the vitality of Zapotec language and culture is a resurgence of value attached to ethnicity which in 1967 I found to be virtually dead. While in the 1930s and 1940s educated Zapotec intellectuals living and working mainly in Mexico City promoted retention of Zapotec language and customs which they, in their comfortable urban nostalgia, elevated to romantic perfection, the people living the language and customs were not so convinced of their value. In 1967 many informants expressed dissatisfaction with the "backwardness" of their community and culture and had strong feelings about the positive value of westernization. In the 1980s, partly through the use of ethnicity to promote the alternative political party COCEI (Campbell 1990), but also as more young people gained perspective through education and knowledge of a world-wide struggle by indigenous groups to preserve their cultures, Isthmus Zapotecs have come to value anew their language and culture. Although there is no concerted movement outside the political arena, a few young couples today express their ethnicity by naming their children non-Catholic Zapotec names like *Naxheli* (I love you), *Nacanda* (dawn), or *Nisa Guie* (rain). Zapotec remains the first language of every child in San Juan and is still spoken by everyone as the dominant and preferred language. Maybe the next move in valuing and expressing ethnicity will be a reversion to the

---

[8]In 1990 a friend–informant whom I have known since she was a teen-ager came to talk with me about how she could get her husband to quit drinking. She said she was looking for a religion, "any religion that can make him stop drinking." She wept as we talked for more than an hour about how she might get her husband out of alcoholism. Unfortunately, the husband has been unwilling to make a commitment.

A Respected Household Head (1982)

old name for themselves, *Binni Za* (we who speak our language), in preference to the Spanish-imposed designation, Zapotecs, a pattern which has become common among many indigenous groups elsewhere in recent years.

We have noted that San Juan has always changed and it is changing still. With the Mexican government's commitment to make the Salina Cruz refinery one of the largest in the world and their further interest in keeping as many Isthmenians as possible within the PRI fold through more attention to community needs (if the national president keeps his promises), the coming decade may see an acceleration of change as great as any since the sixteenth century. As new alternatives appear and old behavior patterns become less satisfactory, less attractive, and more difficult to follow, it is my hope that the people can preserve those essential values and attitudes that give to Isthmus Zapotec its nobility. Among such values I would include a belief in the essential humanity of every individual, an insistence on the right of every person to maintain her dignity as a human being regardless of ethnic or class differences, respect for the aged, a profound empathy with and concern for ill, dying, and otherwise unfortunate people, an attitude that the sexes are of equal value, tenderness and indulgence toward children, which somehow avoids the pitfalls of excessive permissiveness, and an indomitable independence of spirit.

Glossary

Agua potable: Water purified for household use.
Ahijado: Godchild.
Aire: "Bad" air associated with night and able to cause illness. Elsewhere often called *mal aire*.
Ambulante: Roving, nonpermanent market vendor with no regular space in the market place.
Ayuntamiento: Municipal government.
Baile: Dance.
Barrio: Quarter, neighborhood, subsection of pueblo.
Baul: Wooden trunk, usually with four legs and handsomely carved.
Borracho: Drunken; a drunken man.
Buena gente: Fine people.
Cacao: Cocoa.
Calor: Invisible aspect of recently deceased persons which can cause illness and death by contagion.
Campesino: Peasant farmer.
Campo, el: The fields.
Cantina: Tavern, saloon.
Cantinera: Woman owner or operator of a cantina.
Carnicera: Woman vendor of fresh meat, one of the few types of selling considered to be a specialization.
Carreta: Oxcart.
Cargo: Office, voluntary religious office.
Cebu: Humped breed of cattle introduced from Asia.
Celoso: Jealous.
Chile ancho: A variety of chile pepper.
Choza: Small dwelling of reeds and thatch.
Cohete: Firecracker, rocket.
Comadre: Ritual co-mother.
Comerciante: Merchant or businessman, usually having a number of different sources of income.
Compadrazgo: The institution of co-parenthood.
Compadre: Ritual co-father.
Confianza: Confidence, trust.
Coraje: Anger, illness caused by emotion of anger.
Cordoncillo: An herb often used for curative purposes.
Corredor: Veranda, roofed porch across front of house.
Corresponder: To respond, reciprocate.
Costumbres (las): "The customs," a frequent phrase referring to Zapotec customs, especially those of a ceremonial nature.
Criollo: Local breed of plant or animal.
Cuota: Men's ritual monetary contribution, in 1966 usually $5.
Curandera: Woman curer.
Don: Spanish title of respect for men.
Doña: Spanish title of respect for women.
Ejido: Communal land ownership established after the Mexican Revolution.
Enramada: Thatch-roofed sunshade.

Espanto: Fright, illness caused by fright.

Ex-distrito: Territorial subdivision of state, encompassing but having only partial political jurisdiction over several municipios.

Fletero: Motor-freight hauler, truck driver.

Gringa: A woman from the United States, any foreign woman of European phenotype.

Gueeze´: Pinol, maize-flour gruel; the dry sweetened maize flour alone.

Hectare: An area of land measuring 2.47 acres.

Huipil: Woman's unfitted blouse.

Invitados (los): Invited guests at fiesta.

Istmeño: A native inhabitant of the Isthmus of Tehuantepec.

Jicalpextle: Lacquered gourd bowl, hand-painted with floral designs, a specialty of Chiapa de Corzo, Chiapas. Now expensive and seldom used in Isthmus fiestas.

Juaneco(a): Resident of San Juan Evangelista.

Limosna: Woman's ritual contribution, in 1966 customarily $3.

Machismo: Excessive concern with proving one's maleness.

Madrina: Godmother.

Marimacha: Masculine woman.

Material: Products necessary for quality house construction, including adobe, tile, and plaster.

Mayordomo(a): Sponsor of fiesta.

Mazorca: Unhusked ear of mature maize.

Mestizo: Person bearing national culture, speaking only national language, having no known or recognizable ethnic ties.

Mezcal: Alcoholic beverage made from maguey plant.

Mixa gue´tu´: Death rites, memorial rites for deceased, literally "mass for the dead."

Mole: Red sauce of chile and other condiments served at fiestas.

Monte (el): Literally "the bush," that part of the land not cultivated.

Municipio: Smallest political unit of the Republic of Mexico, somewhat similar to U.S. county.

Muy cerrado: Inhospitable to outsiders, very secretive and inwardly oriented.

Muxe: Man–woman; effeminate man; homosexual man.

Niño(a): Infant or small child.

Nixtamal: Maize soaked in lime water, ready to be ground into coarse dough (masa).

Norte (el): The prevalent strong north wind.

Novio(a): Sweetheart or bridegroom/bride.

Ojo: Evil eye.

Olla: Pottery jar.

Padre: Catholic priest, father.

Padrino: Godparent of child in baptism, communion, or marriage.

Palo: Wood pole or club.

Palacio: City hall.

Panteon: The cemetery. Major Isthmus towns have two or more.

Parque: Town plaza.

Partera: Midwife.

Paseando: Strolling idly about for pleasure and recreation.

Paseo: Promenade around the central square, a traditional courting mechanism of Spain and Latin America.

Peso: Mexican currency valued in 1966–1967 at approximately 8 cents U.S.; in 1990, 3000 pesos was approximately 1 U.S. dollar.

Por civil: By civil ceremony.

Por los dos lados: By both sides; married by both civil and religious rites.

Por robar: Marriage by elopement, by "robbing."

Pozol: Cornmeal-based gruel/soup.

Presidente: Elected head of the municipio government, an office somewhat analogous to U. S. mayor.

Promesa: Vow to a saint.

Pueblo libre: Politically autonomous pueblo.

Pueblo rebelde: A rebellious town or community.

Puesto: Market stall.

Rebozo: Woman's shawl.

Redila: Open stock truck with high slat sides and endgate, used as public transportation to remote areas.

Refresco: Cold beverage, often with fruit base.

Rezador(a): Lay prayer leader.

Sancudo: A small hard-biting mosquito.

Santa mesa: Household shrine; the "saint's table" where men pay their ceremonial fees at fiestas.

Señora: Matron, a married or widowed woman.

Serrano: A person native to the sierra.

Sierra: Mountainous region.

Sin cultura: "Without culture," lacking in social refinement.

Solar: The house lot and all structures thereon.

Soldado: Soldier.

Susto: Fright, illness caused by fright.

Tardecita: Late afternoon and early evening.

Templo: Temple, a non-Catholic religious structure.

Terrenos de labor: Gardens, orchards, and small fields requiring intensive care.

Tesis: Thesis, a word familiar to informants because it is a requirement for a teaching credential in the federal education system.

Tía: Aunt.

Tiendita: Little store.

Todos Santos: All Souls' Day.

Torito: Young ox.

Torta: Small cake, sandwich, bun.

Tortillera: A woman who makes or sells tortillas.

Totopo: An oven-baked tortilla of cracker-like character, speciality of San Juan Evangelista.

Totopera: A woman who makes or sells totopos.

Trabajo: Work

Traje: The hand-embroidered velvet huipil and skirt worn by women on ceremonial and festive occasions. In San Juan it is known as Traje Tehuana.

Tristeza: Sadness.

Turista: Tourist.

Urbano: Municipal bus.

Vallista: A person from the Valley of Oaxaca.

Vela: Literally "candle" but referring to a festival of one evening's duration associated with a longer fiesta.

Viajera: Traveling woman vendor.

Xuana: Principal; barrio headman, formerly a politico-religious office, now only voluntary religious office of 1-year term.

Zandunga: Traditional dance in which men and women circle around each other without touching.

References

Aswad, Barbara C., 1967, "Key and Peripheral Roles of Noble Women in a Middle Eastern Plains Village," *Anthropological Quarterly* 40:139–152.

Blackwood, Evelyn, ed., 1986a, *Anthropology and Homosexual Behavior*. Special issue of the *Journal of Homosexuality*.

Blackwood, Evelyn, 1986b, "Breaking the Mirror: The Construction of Lesbianism and the Anthropological Discourse on Homosexuality," in *Journal of Homosexuality* 11:1–17.

Brown, Judith, 1970, "A Note on the Division of Labor by Sex." *American Anthropologist* 72:1073–1078.

Cajigas Langner, Alberto, 1954, *Monografia de Tehuantepec*. Mexico: Imprenta Manuel Leon Sanchez, S.C.L.

Campbell, Howard, 1990, *Zapotec Ethnic Politics and the Politics of Culture in Juchitan, Oaxaca (1350–1990)*, Doctoral thesis in Anthropology, University of Wisconsin, Madison.

Campbell, Howard, 1989, "The COCEI: Culture, Class and Politicized Ethnicity in the Isthmus of Tehuantepec." *Ethnic Studies Report*, 7(2):36–60.

VIII Censo General de Poblacion, 1960, Tomo II, Mexico, published 1963.

Chagnon, Napoleon A., 1968, *Yanomamo: The Fierce People*. New York: Holt, Rinehart and Winston, Inc.

Covarrubias, Miguel, 1954, *Mexico South: The Isthmus of Tehuantepec*. New York: Alfred A. Knopf. First printing 1946.

Davis, Susan S., 1982, *Patience and Power: Women's Lives in a Moroccan Village*. New York: Schenkman.

Delgado, Agustin, 1961, "La secuencia arqueologica en el Istmo de Tehuantepec," in *Los Mayas del Sur y sus Relaciones con Los Nahuas Meridionales*. VIII Mesa Redonda (1959), Sociedad Mexicana de Antropologia. Mexico.

Elkin, A. P., 1950, Introduction to *Aboriginal Woman* by Phyllis Kayberry. New York: Humanities Press, Inc.

Elmendorf, Mary L., 1971, "The Role of Women as Agents for Peaceful Change." Unpublished paper read at 12th World Conference of the Society for International Development, Ottawa, Canada.

Forster, James R., 1953, "Notas Sobre la Arqueologia de Tehuantepec." *Anales de Instituto Nacional de Antropologia e Historia* 7:77–100. Mexico.

Foster, George M., 1961, "The Dyadic Contract: A Model for the Social Structure of a Mexican Peasant Village," *American Anthropologist* 63:1173–1192.

Foster, George, 1965, "Peasant Society and the Image of Limited Good." *American Anthropologist* 67:2.

Friedl, Ernestine, 1967, "The Position of Women: Appearance and Reality." *Anthropological Quarterly* 40:97–108.

Gay, Jose Antonio, 1980, *Historia de Oaxaca*. Vol. 2, Tomo Primero, 3rd ed. Mexico. First printing 1881.

Gonzalez, Nancie, 1984, "Rethinking the Consanguinial Household and Matrifocality. *Ethnology* 23:1–12.

Gonzalez, Nancie, 1970, "Toward a Definition of Matrifocality," in *Afro-American Anthropology*, Norman Whitten and John Szwed, eds. Glencoe: Free Press.

Goodale, Jane, 1970, *Tiwi Wives,* AES Monograph #50. Seattle: University of Washington Press.

Greenberg, David F., 1986, "Why was the Berdache Ridiculed?" in Blackwood 179–189.

Harris, Marvin, 1971, *Culture, Man, and Nature.* New York: Thomas Y. Crowell Company.

Hart, C.W.M., and Arnold Pilling, 1960, *The Tiwi of North Australia.* New York: Holt, Rinehart and Winston, Inc.

Herdt, Gilbert, ed., 1984, *Ritualized Homosexuality in Melanesia,* Berkeley: University of California Press.

Iturribarria, Jorge Fernando, 1960, "Yagul: Mestizo Product of Mixtecs and Zapotecs." *Boletin* No. 17, *Estudios Oaxaquenos,* John Paddock, ed. Mexico.

Kayberry, Phyllis, 1950, *Aboriginal Woman,* New York: Humanities Press.

Kerns, Virginia, 1983, *Women and the Ancestors: Black Carib Kinship and Ritual,* Chicago: University of Illinois Press.

Lee, Richard B., 1968, "What Hunters Do For a Living or How to Make Out on Scarce Resources," in Richard Lee and Irven DeVore, eds., *Man the Hunter.* Chicago: Aldine Publishing Co.

Lee, Richard B., and Irven DeVore (eds.), 1968, *Man the Hunter.* Chicago: Aldine Publishing Co.

Lockard, Denyse, 1986, "The Lesbian Community: An Anthropological Approach," in Blackwood 1986a, 83–95.

Martin, JoAnn, 1990, "Motherhood and Power: The Production of a Women's Culture of Politics in a Mexican Community." *American Ethnologist* 17:470–490.

Mintz, Sidney, 1969, "Review of *Peasants* by Eric R. Wolf." *American Anthropologist* 71:1136–1139.

Mintz, Sidney W., and Eric R. Wolf, 1950, "An Analysis of Ritual Co-Parenthood." *Southwestern Journal of Anthropology* 341–364. Bobbs-Merrill Reprint A-159.

Money, John and A. Ehrhardt, 1972, *Man and Woman, Boy and Girl: Differentiation and Dimorphism in Gender Identity from Conception to Maturity.* Baltimore: Johns Hopkins University Press.

Ortner, Sherry B., and Harriet Whitehead, eds., 1981, *Sexual Meanings: The Cultural Construction of Gender and Sexuality,* London: Cambridge University Press.

Pillard, Richard C., and James C. Weinrich, 1986, News Report in the *San Francisco Chronicle,* August 1, 1986, from *Archives of General Psychiatry,* v. 42.

Riegelhaupt, Joyce F., 1967, "Saloio Women: An Analysis of Informal and Formal Political and Economic Roles of Portuguese Peasant Women," *Anthropological Quarterly* 40:97–108.1

Rosaldo, Michelle, and Louise Lamphere, eds. 1974, *Woman, Culture, and Society,* Stanford: Stanford University Press.

Rymph, David, n.d., "Cross-Sex Behavior in an Isthmus Zapotec Village." Paper presented at the 73rd Annual Meeting, American Anthropological Association, Mexico City, November 1974.

Selby, Henry A., 1974, *Zapotec Deviance.* Austin: University of Texas Press.

Spindler, George, and Louise Spindler, 1970, "Fieldwork Among the Menomini," in George D. Spindler, ed., *Being an Anthropologist: Fieldwork in Eleven Cultures.* New York: Holt, Rinehart and Winston, Inc.

Starr, Frederick, 1900, *Notes upon the Ethnography of Southern Mexico,* Putnam Memorial Publication Fund.

Stephen, Lynn, 1990, "The Politics of Ritual: The Mexican State and Zapotec Autonomy, 1926–1989," in Lynn Stephen and James Dow, eds., *Class, Politics, and Popular Religion in Mexico and Central America,* 10, Society for Latin American Anthropology Publication Series.

Stevens, Evelyn, 1973, "Marianismo: The Other Face of Machismo in Latin America," in *Female and Male in Latin America*, Ann Pescatello, ed. Pittsburgh: University of Pittsburgh Press.

Tanner, Nancy, 1974, "Matrifocality in Indonesia and Africa and Among Black Americans," in Rosaldo and Lamphere.

Torres de Lagunas, Juan de, 1580, "Descripcion de Teguantepec," in Vargas Rea, ed., *Biblioteca Aportacion Historica*, 1958, Mexico.

Weiner, Annette, 1976, *Women of Value, Men of Renown: New Perspectives in Trobriand Exchange*. Austin: Univ. of Texas Press.

Whitehead, Harriet, 1981, "The Bow and the Burden Strap: A New Look at Institutionalized Homosexuality in Native North America," in Ortner and Whitehead, 80–115.

Wolf, Eric R., 1966, "Kinship, Friendship, and Patron–Client Relations in Complex Societies," in M. Banton, ed., *The Social Anthropology of Complex Societies*, ASA Mon. 4. New York: Frederick A. Praeger, Inc.

Wolf, Eric R., 1967, "Closed Corporate Peasant Communities in Mesoamerica and Central Java," in Jack Potter et al, eds., *Peasant Society: A Reader*, Boston: Little, Brown & Co.

Recommended Readings

Readings selected for particular relevance to this edition of *The Isthmus Zapotecs* are:

Andreas, Carol, 1985, *When Women Rebel: The Rise of Popular Feminism in Peru*, Westport, Conn.: Lawrence Hill & Co.

Bossen, Laurel H., 1984, *The Redivision of Labor: Women and Economic Choice in Four Guatemalan Communities*, Albany: State University of New York.

Chaney, Elsa, 1979, *Supermadre: Women in Politics in Latin America*. Austin: University of Texas Press.

Collier, Jane F., and Michelle Z. Rosaldo, 1981, "Politics and Gender in Simple Societies." In *Sexual Meanings: The Cultural Construction of Gender and Sexuality*. Sherry B. Ortner and Harriet Whitehead, eds. 275–329. Cambridge: Cambridge University Press.

Covarrubias, Miguel, 1954, *Mexico South: The Isthmus of Tehuantepec*. New York: Alfred A. Knopf. A colorful, somewhat romanticized account of Isthmus Zapotecs is part of a description of the entire area and includes notes on several other ethnic groups. The author was a famous Mexican artist who developed a keen interest in pre-Columbian archaeology and artifacts, especially those of the Olmec style.

Davis, Susan, 1982, *Patience and Power: Women's Lives in a Moroccan Village*. New York: Schenkman. Applies the Isthmus Zapotec gender role model to an analysis of women's roles in a Muslim culture.

Etienne, Mona, and Eleanor Leacock, eds., 1980, *Women and Colonization: Anthropological Perspectives*, New York: Bergin. An examination of the role of European colonization in lowering the status of native women around the world.

Friedl, Ernestine, 1975, *Women and Men: An Anthropologist's View*, New York: Holt, Rinehart, and Winston. An anthropological overview of gender roles cross-culturally.

Gil, Lesley, 1990, "Like a Veil to Cover Them: Women and the Pentecostal Movement in La Paz," *American Ethnologist* 17:708–721. An examination of the gender ideology of Peruvian Pentacostalism and why it attracts poor women household heads as converts.

Goodale, Jane, 1970, *Tiwi Wives*. AES Monograph #50. Seattle: University of Washington Press. A reexamination of the roles of Tiwi wives and kinswomen compared with the earlier writings of Hart and Pilling.

Ingham, John M., 1986, *Mary, Michael and Lucifer: Folk Catholicism in Central Mexico*. Austin: University of Texas Press.

Lutz, Catherine, 1990, "The Erasure of Women's Writing in Sociocultural Anthropology," *American Ethnologist* 17:611–627. Statistical analysis of anthropology journal citations by gender and discussion of why women anthropologists are published on a par with men but cited at much lower rates.

Martin, Joann, 1990, "Motherhood and Power: The Production of a Women's Culture of Politics in a Mexican Community." *American Ethnologist* 17(3):470–490. Examines the formation of women's political action groups in a mestizo community in Morelos, Mexico.

Mathews, Holly H., 1985, "We are Mayordomo': A Reinterpretation of Women's Roles in the Mexican Cargo System," *American Ethnologist* 12:285–301.

Parsons, Elsie Clews, 1936, *Mitla, Town of the Souls*. Chicago: University of Chicago Press. Parsons' study remains useful for an understanding of Valley Zapotec culture as it was in the 1930s. The Appendix E is especially helpful on trade goods and trade routes.

Rosaldo, Michelle, and Louise Lamphere, eds., 1974, *Woman, Culture, and Society*. Stanford, Stanford University Press. The classic theoretical work on gender roles cross-culturally.

Stevens, Evelyn P., 1973, "Marianismo: The Other Face of Machismo in Latin America," in *Female and Male in Latin America*, Ann Pescatello, ed., Pittsburgh: University of Pittsburgh Press. Examines the place of women in the folk Catholic belief system of Latin America.

Tanner, Nancy, 1974, "Matrifocality in Indonesia and Africa and Among Black Americans," in Rosaldo and Lamphere. Defines matrifocal culture and compares four cultures which fit her criteria of matrifocality.

Weiner, Annette B., 1976. *Women of Value, Men of Renown: New Perspectives in Trobriand Exchange*. Austin. University of Texas Press. A reexamination of women's roles in the exchange system of the Trobriand Islands, comparing her findings with the numerous publications of the original Trobriand ethnographer, Bronislaw Malinowski.

Whitecotton, Joseph, 1984, *The Zapotecs: Princes, Priests, and Peasants*, Norman: University of Oklahoma Press. Excellent overview of the history and ethnology of all the sub-groups of Zapotec-speaking peoples in Mexico.

Williams, Walter L., 1986, *The Spirit and the Flesh: Sexual Diversity in American Indian Culture*, Boston: Beacon Press. A comprehensive history and ethnology of the place of third gender males in Native American cultures in North America.